GOD
B.C.

GOD
B.C.

ANTHONY PHILLIPS

Chaplain and Fellow, St. John's College, Oxford

With a Foreword by
The Bishop of London

With all good wishes

Anthony Phillips

21. iii. 84

OXFORD LONDON NEW YORK
OXFORD UNIVERSITY PRESS
1977

Oxford University Press, Walton Street, Oxford OX2 6DP
OXFORD LONDON GLASGOW NEW YORK
TORONTO MELBOURNE WELLINGTON CAPE TOWN
IBADAN NAIROBI DAR ES SALAAM LUSAKA ADDIS ABABA
KUALA LUMPUR SINGAPORE JAKARTA HONG KONG TOKYO
DELHI BOMBAY CALCUTTA MADRAS KARACHI

Hardbound edition ISBN 0 19 213959 2
Paperback edition ISBN 0 19 281211 4

Set in Great Britain by Gloucester Typesetting Co. Ltd.
Printed in Great Britain by Billing and Sons, Ltd,
Guildford, London, and Worcester

Foreword

by the Bishop of London

When St. Paul wrote his letters, the gospels had not yet been written and the New Testament did not exist. When therefore he commends the study of the scriptures he is referring to the Old Testament. He tells the young churches, consisting mainly of Gentiles, that the ancient Jewish scriptures are of importance and that God intended them for Christians.

This message is true today. In recent years the Old Testament has been neglected. We need to re-discover what it has to say to us so that it may prove to be profitable in leading God's people along the way to perfection, and the practice of good works.

I warmly commend this book by Dr. Phillips, especially to those who during Lent want to deepen their understanding of the Christian faith.

Gerald London:

For
LUCY

Preface

I wish to thank Dick and Joan Foster for giving me the requisite sanctuary in which to write this book, my pupils for helping me to forge the ideas, and my wife for typing the manuscript. It is an Apologia for my interest in the Old Testament. I hope it will encourage others to a similar interest.

Oxford
September 1976

ANTHONY PHILLIPS

Contents

Introduction

Before the advent of archaeological discovery in the ancient Near East, the Old Testament loomed out of an almost totally unknown past. But once the excavating began, despite some false starts and over-easy conclusions—a tendency still prevalent in some quarters today—growth in knowledge of the languages, ideas, and customs of the various peoples who inhabited this region has been immense. Yet ironically in our own times, despite the illumination that archaeology and modern biblical scholarship have brought to our understanding of the Scriptures, the Old Testament is increasingly little known. Indeed there is a widespread tendency, present even in some university circles, to dismiss the Old Testament as irrelevant to the beliefs of 'man come of age'. The jealous God of Sinai seems to bear little resemblance to the loving Father of the New Testament. The stories of bloody battles, the exultations over defeated enemies, and the prayers for their utter annihilation, cannot be reconciled with the teaching of the Prince of Peace. So a latter-day Marcionism[1] prevails and the Old Testament ceases to feed faith, despite the fact that the continuing history of bloodshed in the name of Christ hardly entitles criticism of ancient Israel.

Paradoxically, part of the current trend of ignoring the Old Testament has been the result of scholarly research itself, for this has shown the immense complexity of the Hebrew Scriptures. No longer can they simply be read from cover to cover as the account of ancient Israel's relationship

---

[1] Marcion was a second-century Christian heretic who rejected the Old Testament on the grounds that the God described there had nothing to do with the loving God of Jesus Christ. His thesis that the Christian Gospel was wholly based on love to the absolute exclusion of law also led him to reject large sections of the New Testament.

with her God. For not only does the material present some
thousand years or more of literary activity, but that material
itself has been the constant subject of addition, rewriting, and
re-editing. So the Pentateuch, once firmly attributed to
Moses, is seen to be the fusion of two literary works dating
from after the exile of the Jews in Babylon (586 B.C.): the
Tetrateuch (Genesis–Numbers) and Deuteronomy, itself the
first book of the Deuteronomic Work (Deuteronomy–2
Kings). The account of how the Tetrateuch reached its
present form, from the first literary strand probably written
in the time of Solomon (c. 961–922 B.C.) to the so-called
Priestly editing after the exile, is itself a complex and contro-
versial subject. Nor is this internal literary development to be
confined to the Pentateuch, for even a prophet's work could
be subject to the same process. So prophecies of Isaiah about
the impending fall of Samaria in 721 B.C. were in his lifetime
reinterpreted as of Jerusalem and then used again long after
his death to apply to the events leading up to the Babylonian
conquest in 586 B.C. This constant reinterpretation of Scripture sprang from the Hebrews' recognition of the word of
God as essentially active, and so to be made real for each
generation in the peculiar situation and problems which
confronted it.

Unarguably the experience of the destruction of Jerusalem
and the exile in Babylon was the most cataclysmic event in
ancient Israel's history, for it questioned her continued existence as the chosen people of God. It is the theological reaction to this appalling calamity which dominates the
Old Testament. For this reason it is essential in reading the
Old Testament to know what is pre- and what is post-exilic
material. And this is by no means obvious. How is the un-
instructed reader to recognize that the creation account in
Genesis 2 set in the garden of Eden comes from the earliest
literary strand, probably written in the reign of Solomon,
while the seven-day account of creation in Genesis 1 is a
concise summary of revolutionary post-exilic theology? Similarly the prophetic messages of those who precede the
disaster of 586 B.C. and of those who follow it are theologically
as different as chalk from cheese. For the post-exilic prophets,

understanding of their God has been radically altered by the events through which they lived. As we shall see when we look at the book of Job, theology in the end must always reflect life as it is.

It is the purpose of this short study, by cutting through, though not ignoring, the welter of scholarly theories, to present the essential 'gospel' of the Old Testament, a 'gospel' which receives its confirmation in the work and words of Jesus Christ. The hope is that this study may lead the reader once more to explore the treasures of ancient Israel's faith, though to do so he will need the aid of commentaries and guides which can go much deeper than this necessarily surface work. But it remains true that without a proper understanding of the Old Testament any interpretation of the New Testament must be defective.

In the first chapter we shall explore pre-exilic Israel's understanding of her God based on her law, and in the second show how, without that law's being revoked, this understanding was radically altered by the experience of the exile. In Chapter 3 we shall examine the essential nature of belief as understood within the Old Testament itself in the book of Job, and in the final chapter we shall show how the strands we have picked out find their fulfilment in the person of Jesus Christ, who acknowledged as his Father the jealous God of Sinai. Where Scripture is quoted, the Revised Standard Version is used: all dates are B.C. unless otherwise stated.

I

The Jealous God

It is the purpose of law to ensure the maintenance of order within society, and when that order has been broken to reconcile the warring parties so that harmony can be restored within the community. But the order laid down for society is the order which those in power can enforce. This will vary enormously according to the political structure of the community. A democracy will in the end only be able to enforce those laws which the people as a whole will to obey. It was not radical reformers but widespread rejection of the existing law which led to the 1967 Abortion Act in Great Britain. But in a totalitarian state, the people have no say in the ordering of society. They must obey the will of those who govern until they can overthrow them. Law, then, cannot automatically be appealed to as an arbiter for righting all wrongs. Law itself can, and frequently does, perpetuate those wrongs. Further, what is order in one country would be considered disorderly in another. A comparison of the racial legislation of the Republic of South Africa with that of the United Kingdom makes this very clear. The legal system of any community is, then, peculiar to that community, and like any national characteristic can tell us much about that community, as to both its political and religious ideologies, and the value it places on the individual within the state.

Ancient Israel's law is no exception to these observations. Nowhere within the Old Testament is any of it attributed to human agency; instead it is seen as the direct revelation of God to his people, reflecting that divine order which he has willed for them. This itself is based on that paradisal ordered existence which God inaugurated at creation and which man by his lawlessness has marred. It is for this reason that Israel's law above all other laws is 'righteous'. It is intended to secure for society *shalom*, true peace and harmony between God and man, and man and his neighbour. Consequently, by studying the content of pre-exilic Israel's law we should be able to discover how ancient Israel understood the nature of the God with whom she had to deal.

But in doing this it must be remembered that Israel's pre-exilic theologians understood her election as conditional: her continued existence depended on her obedience of God's law. This idea is commonly called the Mosaic covenant and can be illustrated like this:

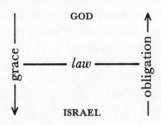

God of his grace had elected Israel and none other to be his chosen people: but in return he had placed obligations on her. Failure to observe these obligations could only lead to divine judgment. The law thus came between Israel and her God and meant that she was always subject to a threat, the threat of total rejection. But in spite of this, the law also acted as the creative machinery whereby Israel could deepen her relationship with the gracious God who had delivered her from Egypt, and who willed her to be his people. By being so connected with the actual covenant relationship, law itself could be seen as part of God's blessing. Israel knew where she stood in relation to her God: her future was in her own hands. Consequently the Deuteronomists could write:

> For what great nation is there that has a god so near to it as the Lord our God is to us, whenever we call upon him? And what great nation is there that has statutes and ordinances so righteous as all this law which I set before you this day?
>
> (Deut. 4:7–8)

(i)

THE DECALOGUE

At the heart of ancient Israel's law lies the Decalogue, the Ten Commandments. These are twice set out in the Old Testament, first at Exod. 20:1–17 and second at Deut. 5:6–21. The two versions are substantially the same except that different motives are given for obedience of the sabbath commandment, and the order of objects which might be coveted varies.[1] But in spite of the very great importance of the Decalogue, scholars have been unable to agree its date and provenance. Tradition holds that the commandments were given to Moses at Sinai, and inaugurated the exclusive covenant relationship between Israel and her God. In the course of time the commandments have undoubtedly suffered considerable expansion and revision from the original short injunctions still found in the prohibitions of murder, adultery, and theft. While it seems certain that the commandments antedate the Davidic monarchy (1000), there is nothing in the content of the original short injunctions which is inapplicable to a desert setting. Even the Hebrew word for 'house' in the tenth commandment could refer to a tent, though since tradition records that the Israelites made bricks in Egypt (Exod. 5:6–19), perhaps they continued to use their expertise at the oasis of Kadesh where they dwelt before entry into Canaan (Deut. 1:46). Further, when we come to look at the legislation of the settlement, we shall see that this seems to be a conscious attempt to integrate the Decalogue into an already existing legal system.

The first and fundamental commandment established Israel's identity as the chosen people of God. Of course the commandment does not rule out the *existence* of other gods: indeed its concern is to ensure that Israel shall have nothing to do with them. She is to acknowledge her God, and her God alone. But the commandment did have two very far-reaching effects. First it ruled out any idea of sexuality in God, for by the terms of the commandment itself, he could

[1] Exod. 20:1–17 is printed as an appendix (pp. 90–91) together with the Deuteronomic versions of the fourth and tenth commandments.

not have a female consort. This is in stark contrast not only to the well known stories of the Greek and Roman gods, but, much more important, to the mythology of Canaanite religion with its strong sexual content designed to ensure the fertility of land and animals. And secondly, the commandment prohibited alliances with the great empires of the ancient Near East. By acknowledging herself a vassal of such an empire, Israel would imply that her God was not strong enough to protect her but had to rely on foreign gods to whom he was himself vassal. From her inception, then, Israel was in a unique theological position in the ancient Near East, both as to the nature of her exclusive relationship with her God and also as to her God's own self-sufficiency.

Since relations with other gods had been ruled out by the first commandment, the 'image' of the second commandment must refer to images of Israel's God, whom she always pictured as a human male figure. Ancient peoples did not think that their god was contained within the image in the sense that if the image was destroyed, so was the god. Rather they thought that wherever they set up an image of their god, they could force him to manifest himself there: they could as it were whistle him up. But Israel's God was never to be controlled by man. He was sovereign, free, other, beyond. Israel had been created for relationship with God, but it was God who had been gracious enough to will that relationship into being and who retained control of how it should be enjoyed. So, unique among ancient peoples, Israel was to have no means of summoning up her God. Consequently all her official shrines remained imageless. And it can hardly be coincidence that in archaeological excavations to date no image of a human male figure has been found.

The same concern for the freedom of Israel's God lies behind the third commandment. This prohibition does not govern blasphemy, for the Israelites believed that if one blasphemed then God would automatically strike one dead; such action amounted to suicide (Job 2:9). There was therefore no need to prohibit it. Nor does it apply to false oaths, for again the Israelites believed that God would take direct action against the offender. The concern of the commandment is the use of the divine name for magical practices. Israel's God had been forced to disclose his name to Moses (Exod. 3) so that in a world populated by many gods, the Israelites would know which God to invoke. Without such knowledge there could be no cult. But this knowledge was not to be abused by trying to exercise power over God. Yet this is what magicians attempt to do. For by the use of special words and actions they seek to persuade divine forces to carry out their will. Such recourse to spells, curses, and other magical practices—the importance of which in the ancient world, fed on fear and superstition, cannot be exaggerated—was thus denied to Israel.

The meaning of the word 'sabbath' remains uncertain, though it is perhaps best understood as 'the day which stops', that is, divides off one set of days from another. Although scholars have sought to discover evidence for the sabbath elsewhere in the ancient Near East, no exact equivalent has been found. This would seem to indicate that while the Hebrews may have known of stopping days used by other peoples, the seven-day week with the regular seventh day of rest must be traced back to ancient Israel and is another unique element in her relationship with her God. It is most likely to be explained as a sign of her political independence from any temporal power, and of her dependence for this freedom on her God alone. In Egypt, the Hebrew slaves would have had no opportunity of regulating their daily work: they had to do what Pharaoh told them. Now Israel's life is to be regulated by the God who willed her to be his special people, and as a further exercise of his grace gave her a regular day of leisure.[1] But originally the sabbath prohibited no more than normal routine work (cf. 2 Kings 4). Only much later was it gradually hedged about with so many restrictions that it became a day of almost total inactivity.

To honour someone means in Hebrew to submit to their authority. In the case of parents this came to be interpreted

[1] While in Deuteronomy 5 the sabbath commandment is connected with slavery in Egypt, in Exodus 20 it is related to the six-day creation account of Genesis 1. This is a later explanation reflecting the importance of the sabbath in post-exilic Israel. Its observance was one of the factors which enabled the exiles to maintain their identity in heathen Babylon.

over the widest possible field, from common assault (Exod. 21:15) to behaviour such as drunk and disorderly conduct (Deut. 21:18–21). But originally the fifth commandment was probably intent on ensuring that children did not renounce their parents' faith. There was to be no freedom of religious choice for those born into Israel. Thus faith in God was preserved from generation to generation. This would have been of vital importance in the desert period when the Hebrews were constantly in touch with peoples of other faiths: but its importance diminished after the establishment of the monarchy (1000), when the worship of Israel's God became the national religion of the new Davidic state. This explains its extension to all sorts of disobedient conduct. None the less, as part of their reaction to Israel's apostasy, the Deuteronomists had to remind their contemporaries that apostates within the family were to be mercilessly rooted out (Deut. 13:6–11).[1]

The first five commandments, therefore, specifically refer to Israel's relationship with her God. They established a unique people whose distinctive nature was assured for all time, a people whose God was in himself entirely self-sufficient, was outside their control, and on whom they were utterly dependent for their freedom to exist as independent of all other nations. Having created Israel, the commandments then go on to protect the individual Israelite, for as a member of the chosen people, each Israelite was of infinite concern to God.

So the sixth commandment prohibits killing within the community—that is, murder. But the commandment has sometimes been used to support various ethical causes involving loss of life. It has in fact nothing to do with pacifism, the abolition of capital punishment, or vegetarianism. Indeed ancient Israel was constantly at war, executed her criminals, and ate meat.

The seventh commandment prohibits adultery, defined as

[1] The law in Deut. 21:18–21 is older than the promulgation of the Deuteronomic laws (621), for it assumes that the local elders still administered justice, whereas following the reform of Jehoshaphat (873–849) professional judges were appointed to handle all such cases (2 Chron. 19:5; cf. Deut. 16:18). See further, p. 9.

sexual intercourse with a married or betrothed woman. A married man was free to have sexual relations with women other than his wife or another married or betrothed woman, though he ran the risk of an action for damages by the father of any girl whose daughter he deprived of her virginity (Exod. 22:16). It has often been thought that adultery was prohibited because the wife represented part of her husband's property. But if this was the case, then it would seem on analogy with the case of seduction of a virgin that the husband would bring an action for damages against the adulterer. But in fact the adulterer was treated as a criminal and executed by the community, the husband playing no part (other than as a possible witness) in the proceedings. Rather the purpose of this commandment probably lies in the need to ensure that a husband might be certain that his children were his own. The importance of this certainty cannot be overestimated in a society which did not believe in life after death, but that one's personality went on in one's children. Indeed the ancient rite in Num. 5:11–31 seems to be a primitive method of ascertaining paternity. The Israelite was to be assured that through his children he continued to have a place in the community of God's chosen people. This illustrates the joy and the importance of seeing one's sons, and sons' sons, four generations (Job 42:16). Death did not destine one to total oblivion.

The eighth commandment merely prohibits theft. But of what? Ancient Israel treated theft of property as a civil offence for which the injured sued for damages (Exod. 22:1–15). But there was also a specific crime of man-theft for which the normal penalty of death was exacted (Exod. 21:16; Deut. 24:7). The situation envisaged was the sale of an Israelite outside the community with almost no hope of his recovery. This was the intended fate of Joseph (Gen. 37). Now our examination of Hebrew law will clearly show that it regarded the protection of persons as in quite a different category from the protection of property. The latter could always be replaced or damages paid by way of compensation. But persons were not replaceable. It would therefore seem probable that the eighth commandment continued the theme of God's concern to protect the *person* of each individual member of the chosen people and therefore governed man-theft. Indeed the practical effect of man-theft was very little different from murder, for ancient Israel believed that once a man left Israelite territory (and this would surely have applied at the oasis of Kadesh too) he automatically came under the influence of other gods (1 Sam. 26:19-20). The Hebrew of Deut. 24:7 in fact describes the man-thief as 'the stealer of life'. A commandment against man-theft would then have been vitally important to the Hebrews during the period in the desert when they were constantly in touch with wandering bedouin; but it would also have retained its importance long after the settlement, in preventing Israelites from selling off their fellow-citizens as slaves to invading foreign powers. Even after the return from exile, Nehemiah had to take action on this issue (5:8).

No legal system can function properly unless it can be assumed that the evidence given in court is the truth. This is recognized by the ninth commandment which prohibits the giving of false evidence.[1] But it is probable that the specific concern of the commandment is the attempt to get a false conviction in a criminal case, leading to the victim's exe-cution—the prescribed penalty for crime in pre-exilic Israel. The classic example of such a judicial murder is the case of Naboth (1 Kings 21). This commandment receives an added importance when it is realized that in Israelite, unlike English, law the accused was presumed guilty until he could prove his innocence. Thus once more the commandment would protect the person of an individual Israelite from loss of his relationship with his God.

But this seems a far cry from the concern of the tenth commandment which in its present form could not in any event be the subject of any legal process. Later, we shall see how the law came to include all sorts of provisions which could never have been enforced by the courts. But is this the case here?

The original short injunction would only have concerned

---

[1] This cannot be called 'perjury' for evidence in ancient Israel was not given under oath.

the house.[1] Let us assume for a moment that it did not merely prohibit coveting but actually depriving the owner of possession. But as we have already noted, and shall see further from our study, Israelite law sharply differentiated in importance offences against persons and offences against property. If our assumption is correct, why should the house alone be considered of such importance that it is specifically brought within the Decalogue?

Now the affairs of the local community were in the hands of 'the elders'. These were the senior male members of each household, the heads of the houses. They acted as spokesmen in the common concerns of the community, the most important of which was the maintenance of order through the administration of justice. To deprive a man of his house would in effect deprive him of his right to exercise his legal role within the community and so strike at the whole democratic basis of Israelite life. This would explain why a commandment on taking a neighbour's house could be found in the Decalogue. But if this was so, why was the wording of the commandment subsequently changed to prohibit coveting?

We know that during the monarchy professional judges were appointed who took over the role of the elders in the administration of justice (2 Chron. 19:5–11). This would have made the original purpose of a commandment forbidding dispossession redundant. It could accordingly be spiritualized by the substitution of 'covet' for an original word for taking possession. At the same time it could have added to it all other property which an Israelite might have obtained by agreement, purchase, or gain, which explains why children are not included in the list. If this reasoning is correct, then the position of the original commandment against dispossession, after the prohibition against false witness, makes very good sense indeed.

In our interpretation of the last five commandments we have suggested that they were specifically designed to protect the person of the individual Israelite rather than his property.

[1] In Deut. 5:21 the wife is placed first, and the house relegated to the second half of the commandment. This reflects the Deuteronomists' innovation in making women members of the covenant community (see p. 27 below).

His position as a member of the covenant community was to be assured. Some may think our interpretation somewhat speculative. It is true there can be no absolute certainty one way or the other. But we shall see that Israel's other pre-exilic law codes regard the protection of property as of very little importance compared with persons. Indeed they take the law on the protection of persons to such an extreme that it comes to include even the exercise of charity, which could never have been enforced by the courts. Yet it is for breach of such laws that Israel is particularly condemned. It would be surprising if this basic difference in the approach to persons and property characteristic of Israelite law, but found nowhere else in any other ancient Near Eastern law code, did not take its origin from the Decalogue itself.

At this stage of our investigation, we can at any rate say that the Decalogue does lead us to one important conclusion about the nature of God. It confirms that while God is jealous for his own position and will not tolerate the acknowledgement of other gods or the improper use of the relationship which he has graciously inaugurated with Israel, he is equally jealous for the protection of those who call upon his name. All that follows will confirm this. Man matters to God.

(ii)

THE BOOK OF THE COVENANT

Both in Exodus and Deuteronomy the Decalogue acts as a prologue to further legislation which the reader is to understand as being deduced from Israel's primary law. This further legislation can then quite properly be attributed to Moses, though historically it is of a much later date. In Exodus this new law is known as The Book of the Covenant (Exod. 20:22 – 23:33) from the use of this phrase in Exod. 24:7. In its original form it is widely held to reflect the conditions of Israel's settlement in Canaan. Indeed many of the precedents are so similar to provisions in other ancient Near Eastern law codes that the Book of the Covenant is clearly drawing on current Canaanite law, itself influenced by those codes.

At first sight the Book of the Covenant seems to lack any coherent pattern, but this is partly due to later additions which have been made to it. But for our purposes we can take the legislation as a whole, for it is all attributed to Israel's God and so reflects his divine nature. What does it tell us about him?

It has not generally been recognized that ancient Israel distinguished between civil wrongs against particular individuals, for which damages were paid to the injured party, and crimes, that is offences against the community, which the community punished in its own name. In pre-exilic Israel this took the form of communal stoning to death outside the criminal's city (1 Kings 21:13).[1] This distinction between criminal and civil offences is amply confirmed by an examination of the legislation of the Book of the Covenant. Once more Israel's law is seen to be in sharp contrast to that of all other ancient Near Eastern legal systems.

Thus a number of precedents in the Book of the Covenant are concerned to distinguish the crime of murder from the civil offence of assault. For instance Exod. 21:18–19 deals with the question of a time limitation against a possible charge of murder:

> When men quarrel and one strikes the other with a stone or with his fist and the man does not die but keeps his bed, then if the man rises again and walks abroad with his staff, he that struck him shall be clear; only he shall pay for the loss of his time, and shall have him thoroughly healed.

Once the injured man has gone for a walk without human aid, his assailant can no longer be charged with murder, even

---

[1] In only one case is mutilation prescribed (Deut. 25:11f.). This is probably to be connected with the destruction of a man's ability to have children. The fact that elsewhere the only penalties laid down are death for crimes and damages for civil offences makes it very doubtful if the celebrated *lex talionis* was an original part of Israelite law. Indeed examination of the three places where it appears shows that in each case it has been later interpolated into the three major legal strands of the Old Testament, namely the Book of the Covenant (Exod. 21:23–5), Deuteronomy (19:21), and the Priestly legislation (Lev. 24:17–21). Its purpose is to stress the principle of compensation, but there is no evidence that it was ever applied literally. While in the case of murder God was seen to have been deprived of the victim's blood, which could only be restored to him through the murderer's execution (Gen. 4:9–10; 2 Sam. 4:11), in other cases of injury appropriate damages would have been required.

if his victim should die on the next day. Instead, damages for assault must now be assessed, which amount to compensation for the victim's enforced idleness and his medical expenses. Since his family would receive no damages if the assault became murder, and the assailant would himself be executed (Exod. 21:12), it was in the interests of all parties that the victim should recover.

But, exceptionally, assault on parents constitutes a crime (Exod. 21:15). This is because it is interpreted as repudiation of parental authority, itself a crime (Exod. 21:17), and prohibited by the fifth commandment.

Although adultery is not mentioned in the Book of the Covenant, we know that it carried the death penalty (Lev. 20:10; Deut. 22:22). But Exod. 22:16–17 provides that seduction of a virgin is to be treated as an injury to her father, whose property she was and who must be compensated by being put in the position he would have been in had there been no injury:

> If a man seduces a virgin who is not betrothed, and lies with her, he shall give the marriage present for her, and make her his wife. If her father utterly refuses to give her to him, he shall pay money equivalent to the marriage present for virgins.

In this case damages simply amount to the bride-price which the father could have expected on his daughter's marriage. He was then no worse off than if the girl had made a marriage with his approval. Normally in a seduction case the couple would have married, but the father had the right to withhold his daughter from her lover and still receive full compensation for the damages he had suffered.

While man-theft, being a crime, carried the death penalty (Exod. 21:16; Deut. 24:7), theft of property led to a civil action for damages which, in the case of theft of animals, were punitive:

> If a man steals an ox or a sheep, and kills it or sells it, he shall pay five oxen for an ox, and four sheep for a sheep. He shall make restitution; if he has nothing, then he shall be sold for his theft.

(Exod. 22:1)

But such damages would only have acted as a deterrent to the poor. This is well brought out by the parable of Nathan told on the occasion of David's adultery with Bathsheba and subsequent murder of Uriah (2 Sam. 12). Indeed this parable can only be understood by recognizing that ancient Israel distinguished between criminal and civil offences.

In highly emotive language, Nathan describes how a rich man with vast flocks and herds seizes a poor man's one ewe lamb to serve up to an unexpected guest. At this David reacts as Nathan expects:

> 'As the Lord lives, the man who has done this deserves to die; and he shall restore the lamb fourfold, because he did this thing, and because he had no pity.'
>
> (2 Sam. 12:5b–6)

Since only the civil law has been broken, the only action which could be taken against the rich man was a suit for damages. Yet because of his riches the punitive damages prescribed by the law in effect left him virtually unpunished. But in David's eyes he deserves to be treated as a criminal and put to death. Yet regretfully he acknowledges the limitations of the legal system. It cannot take into account the moral callousness behind the rich man's heinous action. Damages are all that can be exacted.

But then comes the climax, when Nathan discloses that David himself is the rich man of the parable, and that he has not merely committed a civil offence, but been guilty of the double crime of adultery and murder for which the law demands the death penalty. David in fact only escapes with his life at the direct pardon of God.

We have already seen that murder, adultery, and probably man-theft were all prohibited by the Decalogue because they threatened the person of an individual member of the covenant community. But it is clear from the Book of the Covenant that ancient Israel had an entirely different attitude to property, which in the case of assault included one's body as opposed to one's life-blood or spirit. Property was always expendable and damages could right any wrong to it. But persons could not be so replaced and their position as members of God's chosen people had to be protected by the ultimate sanction of the death penalty. Indeed in its very different attitude to persons and property, the Book of the Covenant would seem to confirm our suggestion that this distinction derives from the Decalogue itself. For it would seem that the conscious differentiation between criminal and civil offences in the Book of the Covenant reflects the process of integrating the distinctive Hebrew law of the Decalogue, brought into Canaan at the time of the settlement, with the indigenous Canaanite law lying behind the civil law precedents. In the changed situation of the settlement, Israel's law was to retain its peculiar nature, for its observance guaranteed her election as God's chosen people.

This is further confirmed by the fact that it is only for offences which can be traced back to the Decalogue that the death penalty is exacted. Thus besides murder (Exod. 21:12), repudiation of parental authority (Exod. 21:15, 17), and man-theft (Exod. 21:16), the Book of the Covenant demands death for sorcery by a woman, bestiality, and sacrificing to other gods (Exod. 22:18–20). Sorcery would, of course, have been prohibited by the third commandment against magical practices. The reason that it is here specifically related to a woman is that originally Israelite law applied only to men, women having no legal status and taking no part in community affairs.[1] Thus, by prohibiting sorcery by a woman, a possible loophole in the existing legislation was closed. Almost certainly bestiality was prohibited because of association with Canaanite rituals. Their aim would have been to attempt physical union with the deity through sacred animals. No such practice was to be found in Israel for her God was to be outside man's control. The prohibition of bestiality is, then, an extension of the intention behind the second and third commandments. Sacrifice to other gods was, of course, prohibited by the first commandment. But here, as the Hebrew makes plain, the Book of the Covenant provides not merely for the death penalty but for the exaction of the ban, that is, that the man and his family should be utterly exterminated so that his name should no

[1] See below, p. 27.

longer be found in Israel. It would be as though he had never existed as part of the chosen people. This was the fate of Achan and his family (Josh. 7) and explains why Naboth's sons were executed with him (2 Kings 9:26). The execution of the criminal would have been seen as a kind of sacrifice to God whose fundamental covenant law had been broken. By executing him through the communal act of stoning, the community as a whole sought to appease God and so ward off the threat of divine punishment falling upon them.

Another conclusion, then, that we can now authoritatively advance is that Israel considered persons more important than property. No doubt there was a great deal more law governing property of which we now know nothing. But the reason for the Old Testament's silence on such law is its theological unimportance. For every codification of Israel's law was undertaken in a theologized form reflecting Israel's understanding of her God. While the Hebrews believed in the goodness of the created order and that it was God's will that they should luxuriate in it, they also recognized that alone in all creation God had made man for communion with himself. It followed then that in God's own law the protection of property could never be considered as of the same fundamental importance as the protection of persons. Further evidence for this overriding concern for persons is to be found in the remarkable legislation on dependent members in Israelite society.

As part of the master's personal property, slaves had, of course, no legal status under the law. Yet Hebrew law both protected them from murder and also gave them civil law rights against their masters in the case of permanent injury:

> When a man strikes his slave, male or female, with a rod and the slave dies under his hand, he shall be punished. But if the slave survives a day or two, he is not to be punished; for the slave is his money.
>
> (Exod. 21:20–1)

> When a man strikes the eye of his slave, male or female, and destroys it, he shall let the slave go free for the eye's sake. If he knocks out the tooth of his slave, male or female, he shall let the slave go free for the tooth's sake.
>
> (Exod. 21:26–7)

Of course the master had every right to chastise his slave, but normally the rod caused no harm (Prov. 23:13). If as a result of his beating the slave was off work for a day or two, then that was the master's loss. The law assumes that no master would want to deprive himself of his own property. But where a slave was literally beaten to death—that is died during the beating or on the same day as the beating—then the master was treated as a murderer and had himself to suffer the normal penalty of death for his savagery. Further, if the beating caused permanent injury, the slave must immediately be released. This amounted in effect to a payment of damages, namely the purchase price of the slave.

These provisions would have applied to any slave whether an Israelite or not. But enslavement of fellow Israelites, usually for debt (Exod. 22:1), though permitted by the law, was none the less regarded as unfortunate. But the law ensured that there should be no permanent enslavement of a fellow Israelite. After six years the slave was to be released, though if he wished he could surrender his right to freedom and remain in his master's service for life (Exod. 21:2–6).

But slaves were not the only dependent members of Israelite society. Widows, orphans, and resident aliens also had to rely on the good nature of the community for their protection, for only adult males had full legal status in ancient Israel and could therefore appeal to the courts for redress:

> You shall not wrong a stranger or oppress him, for you were strangers in the land of Egypt. You shall not afflict any widow or orphan. If you do afflict them, and they cry out to me, I will surely hear their cry; and my wrath will burn, and I will kill you with the sword, and your wives shall become widows and your children fatherless.
>
> (Exod. 22:21–4)

It is worth noting that appeal for charity to the resident alien is based on Egyptian generosity to Israel during her sojourn there.

But in addition to these dependent persons, the Book of the Covenant also enjoins that there should be no exploitation of the poor. Loans are to be made free of interest and the rich are not so to press their legal rights that they make it impossible for the poor to survive. Indeed their charity is to reflect the essential compassion of God himself, whose nature Israel was to represent:

> If you lend money to any of my people with you who is poor, you shall not be to him as a creditor, and you shall not exact interest from him. If ever you take your neighbour's garment in pledge, you shall restore it to him before the sun goes down; for that is his only covering, it is his mantle for his body; in what else shall he sleep? And if he cries to me, I will hear, for I am compassionate.
>
> (Exod. 22:25-7)

Further, this charity is even to extend to animals, whose life-blood, like the blood of man, belongs to Israel's God (Gen. 9:4):

> If you meet your enemy's ox or his ass going astray, you shall bring it back to him. If you see the ass of one who hates you lying under its burden, you shall refrain from leaving him with it, you shall help him to lift it up.
>
> (Exod. 23:4-5)

While natural compassion would lead one to help an animal lost or in distress, if that animal belonged to someone with whom one was in open conflict, then the temptation would be to ignore that animal's plight and so injure one's enemy. But such an attitude at the expense of a defenceless creature is not to be that of Israel.

Thought for both the poor and animals, in this case non-domestic animals, is used to support the law on fallowing in Exod. 23:10-11:

> For six years you shall sow your land and gather in its yield; but the seventh year you shall let it rest and lie fallow, that the poor of your people may eat; and what they leave the wild beasts may eat. You shall do likewise with your vineyard, and with your olive orchard.

Since this provision is intended to provide for the permanent sustenance of the poor and wild beasts, the fallowing would not have taken place universally in one particular year, but would have been by rotation. Similarly the reiteration of the sabbath commandment in Exod. 23:12 specifically enjoins that domestic animals, slaves, and the resident alien should enjoy sabbath rest. There is to be no loophole in the prohibition of regular routine work whereby dependent members of society and animals could be made to work while their masters sat back and rested. However, this did not mean that servants and animals were free to do what they liked (2 Kings 4:22ff.).

But it is clear that many of these charitable laws could not be enforced by the courts. That is why the only sanction offered is direct action by God himself against a disobedient community. But these laws show that any action which caused or furthered personal disorder within the community, even if against those who had no legal rights, was deemed by God to be illegal. Poverty, like widowhood and orphandom, was inevitable, but these were disorderly situations, and everything was to be done to alleviate them. To exploit others' misfortunes was totally alien to the law, and therefore to the character of Israel's gracious God.

Ironically, as the ninth commandment reminds us, the most effective agent of oppression is the maladministration of law. Consequently the Book of the Covenant warns against such practice. If the community cannot rely on the fair and impartial administration of justice, then the law, however fair itself, cannot bring about order:

> You shall not pervert the justice due to your poor in his suit. Keep far from a false charge, and do not slay the innocent and righteous, for I will not acquit the wicked. And you shall take no bribe, for a bribe blinds the officials, and subverts the cause of those who are in the right.
>
> (Exod. 23:6–8)

It is, then, vital to the survival of an ordered society that those who have power should be incorruptible and exercise it impartially. Without such an assurance, a chaotic situation would soon emerge as those in authority sought to exploit their office for their own gain.

We have already seen that in addition to duties towards God, there are also duties towards one's neighbour. But the

Book of the Covenant shows that these neighbourly duties extend far beyond that which can be legally enforced through the courts. But because, as we have also already recognized, persons matter more than property, those who have not, or for some reason are deficient in property, have a right to support from those who have. Charity is part of law because it helps to restore that order which God wills and which law maintains. It is for this reason that it was of such concern to the pre-exilic prophets.

(iii)

THE PROPHETIC PROTEST

It would seem that from her earliest days in Canaan prophets were active in the religious life of Israel, but it was with the eighth century that the prophetic movement reached its full fruition with the work of Amos, Hosea, Micah, and Isaiah. For it was these prophets who first proclaimed in devastatingly unambiguous terms that if Israel continued to disobey her God, then she would forfeit her election as his chosen people. So Amos wrote:

> You only have I known
>   of all the families of the earth;
> therefore I will punish you
>   for all your iniquities.

(3:2)

Although much of the prophets' charges against Israel concerned her apostasy, this was by no means the full extent of their complaint. For alongside the accusation that the chosen people had failed to maintain the exclusive relationship with their God, was the parallel complaint that justice was being perverted and the dependent in society exploited. Israel's election depended not just on the faithful practice of her religion, but also on her social attitudes to those who had no means of protecting themselves. Indeed one of the most striking aspects of the prophetic protest was the recognition that to go through the motions of religious practice was worthless if subsequent action showed that those practices in fact lacked any content. For the prophets, faith and works were not alternatives but represented the two sides of the coin known as true religion. And it appears from the prophetic books that the Israelites were excessively zealous in carrying out their religious duties. So with heavy irony Amos, parodying a call to worship, writes:

> Come to Bethel, and transgress;
>   to Gilgal, and multiply transgression;
> bring your sacrifices every morning,
>   your tithes every three days;
> offer a sacrifice of thanksgiving of that which is leavened,
>   and proclaim freewill offerings, publish them;
>   for so you love to do, O people of Israel!
>
> (4:4-5)

In doing the very things that were ordained by their religion as religious duties, the Israelites were in fact sinning, for their actions outside their worship showed that they had no real understanding of the nature of the God whom they sought to please. How could he accept the gifts of those who at the same time exhibited wanton callousness to the deprived in their community? And the fact that the gifts offered were far more generous than the law prescribed made no difference. Indeed their sacrifices, properly designed to bring about communion between God and men, had precisely the opposite effect. So time and again the prophets made it clear why Israel's worship must be rejected:

> I hate, I despise your feasts,
>   and I take no delight in your solemn assemblies.
> Even though you offer me your burnt offerings and cereal
>   offerings,
>   I will not accept them,
> and the peace offerings of your fatted beasts
>   I will not look upon.
> Take away from me the noise of your songs;
>   to the melody of your harps I will not listen.
> But let justice roll down like waters,
>   and righteousness like an everflowing stream.
>
> (Amos 5:21-4)

A society which was openly and unashamedly disorderly

could, by the very nature of the God who had created all to
be in order, have no place in his scheme of things and must
therefore be utterly rejected.

But the prophets were not against sacrifice itself. It is true
that Amos makes God ask:

> Did you bring to me sacrifices and offerings the forty years
> in the wilderness, O house of Israel?
>
> (5:25)

And this question seems to expect a negative answer. But this
isolated verse must be considered alongside other prophetic
passages. For instance in condemning every aspect of Israel's
religious life, Isaiah writes:

> When you spread forth your hands,
>   I will hide my eyes from you;
> even though you make many prayers,
>   I will not listen;
>   your hands are full of blood.
>
> (1:15)

But no one supposes that the prophets rejected prayer. Yet
prayer is treated by Isaiah in exactly the same way as
sacrifice. Isaiah's point is that any religious practice is
worthless if it is not accompanied by appropriate social and
charitable action:

> Wash yourselves; make yourselves clean;
>   remove the evil of your doings
>   from before my eyes;
> cease to do evil,
>   learn to do good;
> seek justice,
>   correct oppression;
> defend the fatherless,
>   plead for the widow.
>
> (1:16–17)

An explanation for Amos 5:25 may be found in the
treatment of sacrifice by the seventh-century prophet
Jeremiah. Once more irony is used to condemn Israel's
religious practice. Jeremiah argues that instead of offering
any of the sacrificial meat to God, it would be better for the

worshippers to eat it themselves. At least they would get a good square meal, whereas it would be wasted on God who was bound to reject it:

> Thus says the Lord of hosts, the God of Israel: 'Add your burnt offerings to your sacrifices, and eat the flesh. For in the day that I brought them out of the land of Egypt, I did not speak to your fathers or command them concerning burnt offerings and sacrifices. But this command I gave them, "Obey my voice, and I will be your God, and you shall be my people; and walk in all the way that I command you, that it may be well with you".'
>
> (7:21–3)

The distinctive element in the bringing into being of Israel in the exodus from Egypt was not commands about sacrifice, but rather the injunction to keep the divine law given at Sinai. It was on obedience to this that Israel's continued covenant relationship with her God depended. Sacrifice, then, however much it cost the worshipper, was bound to be rejected unless it was accompanied by right action within the community:

> 'With what shall I come before the Lord,
>   and bow myself before God on high?
> Shall I come before him with burnt offerings,
>   with calves a year old?
> Will the Lord be pleased with thousands of rams,
>   with ten thousands of rivers of oil?
> Shall I give my first-born for my transgression,
>   the fruit of my body for the sin of my soul?'
> He has showed you, O man, what is good;
>   and what does the Lord require of you
> but to do justice, and to love kindness,
>   and to walk humbly with your God?
>
> (Mic. 6:6–8)

Shalom—peace, harmony—between God and man is impossible where no *shalom* exists between man and his neighbour. Religious practice can never act as a cloak to hide society's ills. It is no wonder that the prophetic protest found such a ready echo in Victorian England and blossomed again in the Christian Socialist movement.

Because Israel's election rested on her obedience to God's law, the prophets framed their charge against Israel in terms of a lawsuit. So God appears as the plaintiff and formally accuses her. Her guilt is all too apparent from the lack of life all around:

> Hear the word of the Lord, O people of Israel;
>> for the Lord has a controversy with the inhabitants of the land.
> There is no faithfulness or kindness,
>> and no knowledge of God in the land;
> there is swearing, lying, killing, stealing, and committing adultery;
>> they break all bounds and murder follows murder.
> Therefore the land mourns,
>> and all who dwell in it languish,
> and also the beasts of the field,
>> and the birds of the air;
>> and even the fish of the sea are taken away.
>
> (Hos. 4:1–3)

On another occasion God appeals to the oldest elements in creation to act as judges in his plea against his people. They had witnessed his gracious act in selecting Israel and in protecting her in her journey to the promised land. Let them now decide if he is right to reject her:

> Hear what the Lord says:
> Arise, plead your case before the mountains,
>> and let the hills hear your voice.
> Hear, you mountains, the controversy of the Lord,
>> and you enduring foundations of the earth;
> for the Lord has a controversy with his people,
>> and he will contend with Israel.
> 'O my people, what have I done to you?
>> In what have I wearied you? Answer me!
> For I brought you up from the land of Egypt,
>> and redeemed you from the house of bondage;
> and I sent before you Moses,
>> Aaron, and Miriam.
> O my people, remember what Balak king of Moab devised,
>> and what Balaam the son of Beor answered him,

and what happened from Shittim to Gilgal,
    that you may know the saving acts of the Lord.'
                                                (Mic. 6:1-5)

It is lack of justice within the elect community which
particularly concerns the prophets. This does not just mean
that the legal system is corrupt, though this was certainly
part of the complaint. But justice is a wider concept than the
mere administration of law through the courts. It governs all
right relations in society. That the poor are exploited or that
dependent members of society go without is equally lack of
justice. To keep the law in ancient Israel was not just a
matter of not breaking certain injunctions: it also contained
the positive duty to make sure that there should be no one in
need. Where disorder had entered into the community—
whether or not through the sufferer's own fault—society
as a whole had a duty as far as possible to eradicate it, and
if that was impossible, to mitigate any suffering that did
occur. The prophets' charge was that Israel was in fact ex-
ploiting it:

Thus says the Lord:
'For three transgressions of Israel,
    and for four, I will not revoke the punishment;
because they sell the righteous for silver,
    and the needy for a pair of shoes—
they that trample the head of the poor into the dust of the
        earth,
    and turn aside the way of the afflicted.'
                                                (Amos 2:6-7a)

Inevitably such action brings God's judgment, his rejection
of his people:

And I said:
Hear, you heads of Jacob
    and rulers of the house of Israel!
Is it not for you to know justice?—
    You who hate the good and love the evil,
who tear the skin from off my people,
    and their flesh from off their bones;
who eat the flesh of my people,
    and flay their skin from off them,

and break their bones in pieces,
    and chop them up like meat in a kettle,
    like flesh in a cauldron.
Then they will cry to the Lord,
    but he will not answer them;
he will hide his face from them at that time,
    because they have made their deeds evil.

                      (Mic. 3:1–4)

Indeed, for Micah the whole of Israelite society is corrupt.
The very officers who should be ensuring her orderly existence before God are concerned only to amass personal
fortunes. Judgment must fall:

Hear this, you heads of the house of Jacob
    and rulers of the house of Israel,
who abhor justice
    and pervert all equity,
who build Zion with blood
    and Jerusalem with wrong.
Its heads give judgment for a bribe,
    its priests teach for hire,
    its prophets divine for money;
yet they lean upon the Lord and say,
    'Is not the Lord in the midst of us?
    No evil shall come upon us.'
Therefore because of you
    Zion shall be ploughed as a field;
Jerusalem shall become a heap of ruins,
    and the mountain of the house a wooded height.

                  (Mic. 3:9–12)

And this perversion of justice was all at the expense of those
who could least afford it:

Your princes are rebels
    and companions of thieves.
Every one loves a bribe
    and runs after gifts.
They do not defend the fatherless,
    and the widow's cause does not come to them.

                    (Isa. 1:23)

Corruption, then, was prevalent everywhere in Israelite life

and the business community was no exception. Forced to
obey the sabbath law, they longed for it to be over so that
they could get back to their crooked practices:

> Hear this, you who trample upon the needy,
>   and bring the poor of the land to an end,
> saying, 'When will the new moon be over,
>   that we may sell grain?
> And the sabbath,
>   that we may offer wheat for sale,
> that we may make the ephah small and the shekel great,
>   and deal deceitfully with false balances,
> that we may buy the poor for silver
>   and the needy for a pair of sandals,
>   and sell the refuse of the wheat?'
>
> (Amos 8:4–6)

The law given to Israel to make hers the unique people of
God—unique in their exclusive allegiance to him and unique
in their society which was to mirror his gracious nature—was
everywhere being turned on its head:

> Do horses run upon rocks?
> Does one plough the sea with oxen?
> But you have turned justice into poison
>   and the fruit of righteousness into wormwood.
>
> (Amos 6:12)

The eighth-century prophets saw their ministry vindicated in
the destruction of the northern kingdom[1] by the Assyrians in
721. A similar fate for southern Judah was only averted by
the reforms of Hezekiah (715–687) (2 Kings 18). But Israel's
disobedience continued. A final attempt to avert God's
inevitable judgment came when, following the discovery of a
law book in the temple (621), Josiah (640–609) instituted the
Deuteronomic reform (2 Kings 22–3).

---

[1] On the death of Solomon (c. 922), the northern tribes under Jeroboam I
rebelled against the Davidic dynasty and founded the separate kingdom of
Israel (1 Kings 12) whose capital became Samaria (1 Kings 16:24). The
southern kingdom of Judah continued to be ruled by the Davidic dynasty from
Jerusalem.

DEUTERONOMY

Although the book of Deuteronomy reached its present form after the exile, the Deuteronomic laws (12–26, 28) are pre-exilic. It is usually held that these were contained in the law book discovered in Josiah's reign and formed the basis of his reform. The laws themselves make two far-reaching innovations. In the first place they provide for the centralization of all worship at Jerusalem, which led to the consequent destruction of all other shrines. And secondly they make women liable under the law. Before the reform only men had full legal responsibility.

But supporting our interpretation of the Decalogue, and confirming what we have already found in the Book of the Covenant, the most striking element in the Deuteronomic laws, which are of considerable length, is their total lack of interest in the protection of property. There is in fact no concern at all with civil offences other than the incidental discussion of the amount of damages to be paid for a husband's false accusation that his wife had lost her virginity before marriage (22:19), and the standardization of damages payable for seduction of a virgin (22:28–9). Instead, the Deuteronomic laws have two main objectives—to ensure that Israel remains loyal to her God and that charity continues to be exercised in favour of dependent members of society.

Undoubtedly both political and religious motives led Josiah to centralize worship at Jerusalem. Thereby the king was able to exercise total personal control over all Israel's cultic practices. Nothing could now go on of which he was not aware, and which might threaten his own election (cf. 2 Sam. 7) or the election of his people. Further, the Deuteronomic laws provided that whenever apostasy occurred, the offenders were to be unhesitatingly rooted out and destroyed (13). No one was to show them any pity. They threatened the whole existence of the chosen people.

Behind the Deuteronomic laws lies the view that it was through the taking-over of so much Canaanite religious practice that the purity of Israel's religion became contaminated. Had the Canaanites been entirely eliminated at the time of the Hebrews' entry into the land, then Israel would never have been tempted into their abominable heathen ways and her election threatened. This is most clearly seen in the laws on warfare, where, in contrast to the treatment to be meted out to the cities of foreign nations, the inhabitants of the Canaanite cities are to be totally annihilated:

> But in the cities of these peoples that the Lord your God gives you for an inheritance, you shall save alive nothing that breathes, but you shall utterly destroy them, the Hittites and the Amorites, the Canaanites and the Perizzites, the Hivites and the Jebusites, as the Lord your God has commanded; that they may not teach you to do according to all their abominable practices which they have done in the service of their gods, and so to sin against the Lord your God.
>
> (20:16–18)

Thus a number of Deuteronomic laws seem to be deliberately dissociating Israel from Canaanite customs and practices (cf. 14; 18: 9–14; 21:22–3; 22:5; 23:17–18).

But this anti-Canaanite reaction is a decidedly one-sided assessment, for the influence of Canaanite religion and ideas was by no means entirely negative. For what in fact occurred after the Hebrews entered Canaan was that their concept of God as one who had revealed himself to them in specific historical events was fused with indigenous Canaanite ideas of a god who governed nature and fertility. Thus Israel came to realize that her God was not just a tribal deity who protected her in her military encounters, but was also lord of creation which he continued to control. It is true that there were some puritan sects among the Israelites who rejected everything Canaanite, the Nazarites (Amos 2) and Rechabites (Jer. 35), but as the Psalter with its considerable debt to Canaanite worship indicates, they were not typical of orthodox Israelite theology. Thus the Deuteronomic assessment should be compared with that of Hosea. While the prophet unhesitatingly condemns the excesses of Canaanite religious practice, including the treatment of Israel's God as if he were a mere fertility deity like the Canaanite Baal, he none the less uses Canaanite theological ideas concerning nature and fertility to reinterpret Israel's religion for his contemporaries.

In spite of the seriousness of the fate which awaits Israel for her apostasy, the Deuteronomic laws are not confined to injunctions against such action. Remarkably, they show almost equal concern for the exercise of charity, though the provisions enjoining this would have been impossible to enforce by the courts.

Thus Deuteronomy reiterates the law about the release of Hebrew slaves after six years' service, though now, in contrast to the Book of the Covenant (Exod. 21:2–6), it directs that the master must provide lavishly for the slave to start out on his new life:

> And when you let him go free from you, you shall not let him go empty-handed; you shall furnish him liberally out of your flock, out of your threshing floor, and out of your wine press.
>
> (15:13–14a)

Evidently under the earlier law, slaves who were well treated had felt reluctant to exchange security without freedom for freedom without security. Now the slave was to be encouraged to claim his release by having sufficient provided for his immediate future well-being.

Deut. 23:15–16 lays down that a runaway slave shall not be handed over to his master:

> You shall not give up to his master a slave who has escaped from his master to you; he shall dwell with you, in your midst, in the place which he shall choose within one of your towns, where it pleases him best; you shall not oppress him.

No mention is made of the slave's nationality, but it seems probable that the law relates to foreign slaves for whom extradition had been claimed (cf. 1 Kings 2:39f.). On humanitarian grounds such slaves are to be allowed to remain in Israel. Such a provision is in sharp contrast to other ancient Near Eastern law codes and state treaties, which usually provided for extradition.

Debt was the chief cause of slavery, but Deut. 15:1–11 enacts that every seventh year the debts of all Israelites, but not of foreigners, are to be cancelled:

At the end of every seven years you shall grant a release. And this is the manner of the release: every creditor shall release what he has lent to his neighbour; he shall not exact it of his neighbour, his brother, because the Lord's release has been proclaimed. Of a foreigner you may exact it; but whatever of yours is with your brother your hand shall release.

(15:1–3)

The type of debt here envisaged involved a loan in return for the pledge of a person as security, who on failure to repay the loan was taken by the creditor who used his services as compensation. Thus if a loan had not been paid back by the year of release, it could not subsequently be recovered and anyone who had been seized as pledge would have been released. Further, the Deuteronomic law enjoined that even if the year of release was imminent, Israelites were still to lend generously to their fellow citizens in need:

Take heed lest there be a base thought in your heart, and you say, 'The seventh year, the year of release is near,' and your eye be hostile to your poor brother, and you give him nothing, and he cry to the Lord against you, and it be sin in you. You shall give to him freely, and your heart shall not be grudging when you give to him; because for this the Lord your God will bless you in all your work and in all that you undertake. For the poor will never cease out of the land; therefore I command you, You shall open wide your hand to your brother, to the needy and to the poor, in the land.

(15:9–11)

It is interesting to note that while verse 11 realistically acknowledges that the people of Israel will always have the poor among them, verses 4–5 argue that poverty within the community is the result of disobedience to the law of charity:

But there will be no poor among you (for the Lord will bless you in the land which the Lord your God gives you for an inheritance to possess), if only you will obey the voice of the Lord your God, being careful to do all this commandment which I command you this day.

Disorder breeds disorder. It is in the end in the interests of those who have that no one should be in distress. For widespread poverty can only lead to growing discontent and

eventually to conflict and violence. Hebrew law was designed
to prevent this. Deuteronomy also repeats the law of the Book
of the Covenant (Exod. 22:25) that loans to fellow Israelites
were to be free of interest (23:19–20).

Further provisions to protect the poor are contained in the
laws concerning the seizing of a millstone as pledge (24:6),
the return at night of a cloak taken in pledge (24:12–13), and
the payment of wages daily (24:14–15). All these laws would
have prevented severe hardship to the poor.

Deuteronomy also seeks to protect and make provision for
the widow, orphan, and resident alien:

> You shall not pervert the justice due to the sojourner or to
> the fatherless, or take a widow's garment in pledge; but you
> shall remember that you were a slave in Egypt and the Lord
> your God redeemed you from there; therefore I command
> you to do this.
>
> When you reap your harvest in your field, and have
> forgotten a sheaf in the field, you shall not go back to get it;
> it shall be for the sojourner, the fatherless, and the widow;
> that the Lord your God may bless you in all the work of your
> hands. When you beat your olive trees, you shall not go over
> the boughs again; it shall be for the sojourner, the fatherless,
> and the widow. When you gather the grapes of your vine-
> yard, you shall not glean it afterward; it shall be for the
> sojourner, the fatherless, and the widow. You shall remember
> that you were a slave in the land of Egypt; therefore I
> command you to do this.
>
> (24:17–22)

As a basis for this exercise of charity, appeal is again made
to Israel's slavery in Egypt. But it is worth noting the change
in the motive of the appeal. No longer is this to the generosity
of the Egyptians (cf. Exod. 22:21), but rather to the generosity of God who rescued Israel from her appalling state of
servitude. As he had of his own free will acted towards her,
so she is to act towards the less fortunate members in her own
society.

But as a result of the Deuteronomic reform itself, a new
class of dependent persons entered Israel's society. These
were the country Levites who, through the destruction of all

shrines other than the sanctuary at Jerusalem, found themselves without any means of livelihood. Though the Deuteronomic law (18:6ff.) provided that these dispossessed clergy
were entitled to come to Jerusalem and take part in worship
there and so secure their livelihood, the Jerusalem priesthood
prevented this (2 Kings 23:9). Consequently alongside the
widow, orphan, and resident alien, they became entitled to
charitable support:

> And you shall not forsake the Levite who is within your
> towns, for he has no portion or inheritance with you.
> At the end of every three years you shall bring forth all the
> tithe of your produce in the same year, and lay it up within
> your towns; and the Levite, because he has no portion or
> inheritance with you, and the sojourner, the fatherless, and
> the widow, who are within your towns, shall come and eat
> and be filled; that the Lord your God may bless you in all
> the work of your hands that you do.
>
> (14:27–9)

Deuteronomy even extended its laws on charity to include
travellers, who were expressly permitted to sustain themselves
from the crops through which they passed on their journey
(cf. Matt. 12:1), but were forbidden to take anything away
with them:

> When you go into your neighbour's vineyard, you may eat
> your fill of grapes, as many as you wish, but you shall not put
> any in your vessel. When you go into your neighbour's
> standing grain, you may pluck the ears with your hand, but
> you shall not put a sickle to your neighbour's standing grain.
>
> (23:24–5)

Further, the Deuteronomic laws on animals have long been
recognized for their remarkable humanitarianism (22:1–4,
6–7, 10; 25:4).

Finally, Deuteronomy, like the Book of the Covenant
(Exod. 23:6–8), emphasizes the importance of the reliability
of the administration of justice:

> You shall appoint judges and officers in all your towns which
> the Lord your God gives you, according to your tribes; and
> they shall judge the people with righteous judgment. You

shall not pervert justice; you shall not show partiality; and
you shall not take a bribe, for a bribe blinds the eyes of the
wise and subverts the cause of the righteous. Justice, and only
justice, you shall follow, that you may live and inherit the
land which the Lord your God gives you.

(16:18–20)

We find, then, that our further conclusions about the
jealous God of Sinai drawn from the Decalogue and the
Book of the Covenant have been confirmed. He is concerned
not only for his exclusive worship but also for the welfare of
the individual Israelite, and that concern, by appealing to
charity, goes far beyond law which the courts can enforce.
But the protection of personal property is not an overriding
interest of his. Indeed the laws of charity show that such
property is held for the welfare of the community at large and
that those who have not sufficient are entitled to claim from
those who have. For all members of the chosen people have
the right to luxuriate in the land of milk and honey which
God has given them.

Examination of the phrase 'jealous God' indicates in fact
that it is only used where God sees his exclusive relationship
with Israel threatened by her acknowledgement of other gods
(Exod. 20:5; Deut. 4:24; 5:9; 6:15). God *is* jealous for that
relationship. He has of his grace created it and it is through it
that he can manifest his character to the world. Without
Israel, how will men ever know his nature? And that nature
is seen in his law, based not on preserving the rights of those
who have, but in ensuring the welfare of all.

(v)

JUDGMENT

But the Deuteronomic reform was short-lived, and in 586
judgment fell on disobedient Israel when the Babylonians
conquered and sacked Jerusalem. The enormity of the
disaster cannot be exaggerated. As a result the temple, the
meeting place of God and his people, lay in ruins, the king
and leading citizens were taken into exile, and Israel herself
was absorbed into the Babylonian empire:

How lonely sits the city
 that was full of people!
How like a widow has she become,
 she that was great among the nations!
She that was a princess among the cities
 has become a vassal.

(Lam. 1:1)

But this was not all: according to Israel's theologians, it was
not Babylonian military prowess which had brought these
catastrophic events upon Israel: it was her own God. He
alone had secured her defeat and devastation, thereby
indicating that his relationship with her was at an end. At
last the jealous God had acted. The threat present within the
Mosaic covenant had been carried out. No longer was God
prepared to call his own those who so openly flouted the
principles of his divine nature. Israel had in effect judged
herself. She had preferred disorder to order and consequently
lay in ruins. Now even the assurance of the presence of God
given to Israel through the temple had been removed. She
was forced to enter the dark abyss, the silent unknown.
Israel as she had been was dead. But one must die to live: it is
in the dark abyss, the silent unknown, that the real issues of
life are decided. It is there that men commit suicide or express
faith—faith in the God who remains agonizingly absent, and
who can in fact only be present again through the declaration
'In spite of . . . , I believe.' Such was Israel's choice.

2

The Illogical God

THE DEUTERONOMISTS

The Deuteronomists were the first group of theologians to attempt to come to terms theologically with the apparent absolute judgment of God on Israel. Between 560 and 540 they published their Work (Deuteronomy – 2 Kings) in which they sought first to explain why the disaster had occurred, and secondly to look at the possibility of any future for Israel. For the Deuteronomists it was not difficult to pinpoint Israel's failure. She had broken the exclusive covenant relationship with her God inaugurated by Moses on Mount Horeb (the Deuteronomic name for Sinai), and for her apostasy she had been condemned.

But in spite of the undoubted justice of God's judgment upon Israel, the Deuteronomists could not bring themselves to believe that it could be final. Against their own threat theology, they yet envisaged the hope that the gracious God might again lead his people back across the Jordan to the promised land: there might yet be a second exodus. But this could only happen if defeated and exiled Israel remained loyal to her God. Hence the continued importance of the law. It was obedience to this alone which secured God's blessing.

The publication of the Deuteronomic Work was probably inspired by the release of the exiled king Jehoiachin from prison in Babylon in 561 (2 Kings 25:27), for this is the last event recorded in the history. Undoubtedly the king's release caused a wave of excitement to pass throughout

Judaism both in Babylon and Palestine. Was this the prelude
to another mighty act of Israel's God whereby he would
deliver his people from the oppressor so that they might enjoy
their unique relationship with him in the land he had chosen
for them?

Faced with the implementation of God's judgment through
Israel's disobedience of the law, the Deuteronomists offer no
new theological assessment of Israel's relationship with her
God. Their theology continues to be centred on the Mosaic
covenant concept. Failure to obey the law would again lead
to absolute judgment. Thus the Deuteronomists did not
consider that their understanding of their God might be in
any way defective. Instead, they place any hope there might
be in an illogical act of divine mercy—that, as it were, the
gramophone record might be played all over again. Can the
God who had cherished them for so long and given to them
so richly really sever relations with them for all time? Long
before, Hosea had pondered the same question:

> How can I give you up, O Ephraim!
>   How can I hand you over, O Israel!
> How can I make you like Admah!
>   How can I treat you like Zeboiim!
> My heart recoils within me,
>   my compassion grows warm and tender.
> I will not execute my fierce anger,
>   I will not again destroy Ephraim;
> for I am God and not man,
>   the Holy One in your midst,
>   and I will not come to destroy.

(11:8–9)

(ii)

JEREMIAH

But one theologian contemporary with the Deuteronomists
reached a very different conclusion. Like them, Jeremiah
saw that Israel's widespread disregard of God's law made his
judgment inevitable:

Will you steal, murder, commit adultery, swear falsely, burn incense to Baal, and go after other gods that you have not known, and then come and stand before me in this house, which is called by my name, and say, 'We are delivered!'—only to go on doing all these abominations? . . . And now, because you have done all these things, says the Lord, and when I spoke to you persistently you did not listen, and when I called yõu, you did not answer, . . . I will cast you out of my sight, as I cast out all your kinsmen, all the offspring of Ephraim.

(7:9–10, 13, 15)

But he had also recognized that if there was to be a future for Israel then her relationship with her God would have to be on a different footing. The Mosaic covenant was a straight arrangement between Israel and her God, so that no matter what individuals did within the community, the whole community was liable for any breach of law. Jeremiah recognized that such an arrangement would inevitably bring doom upon Israel: what was required was a situation in which the individual himself decided his own fate before his God. Indeed the present arrangement hardly did credit to the nature of Israel's God, who specifically based his relationship with her on justice and righteousness. For when judgment fell, both innocent and guilty were indiscriminately punished. Consequently Jeremiah proclaimed that when Israel was restored—and of this he had no doubt as his purchase of some family land confirms (Jer. 32)—her relationship with her God would be on a very different basis. Communal liability would be abolished and instead a man would be liable only for what he himself did wrong. In other words, the new Israel would consist of those people who individually kept the law:

Behold, the days are coming, says the Lord, when I will sow the house of Israel and the house of Judah with the seed of man and the seed of beast. And it shall come to pass that as I have watched over them to pluck up and break down, to overthrow, destroy, and bring evil, so I will watch over them to build and to plant, says the Lord. In those days they shall no longer say:

'The fathers have eaten sour grapes,
   and the children's teeth are set on edge.'
But every one shall die for his own sin; each man who eats
sour grapes, his teeth shall be set on edge.

(31:27–30)

This radical restructuring of Israel's responsibility before
God by abolishing communal liability would inevitably
result in the replacement of the Mosaic covenant by a totally
new relationship, which Jeremiah goes on to describe. His
prophecy thus marks the transition from Israel's pre-exilic
to her post-exilic theology:

Behold, the days are coming, says the Lord, when I will make
a new covenant with the house of Israel and the house of
Judah, not like the covenant which I made with their fathers
when I took them by the hand to bring them out of the land
of Egypt, my covenant which they broke, though I was their
husband, says the Lord. But this is the covenant which I will
make with the house of Israel after those days, says the Lord:
I will put my law within them, and I will write it upon their
hearts; and I will be their God, and they shall be my people.

(31:31–3)

The old covenant written externally on two stone tablets
and placed in the ark, which bound the whole community
collectively to joint obedience to God, is at an end. Instead
the law is to be a matter of individual obedience—the
covenant relationship is to be with those whose hearts are for
God, no matter what the rest of the people do. So Jeremiah
concludes:

And no longer shall each man teach his neighbour and each
his brother, saying, 'Know the Lord,' for they shall all know
me, from the least of them to the greatest, says the Lord; for
I will forgive their iniquity, and I will remember their sin no
more.

(31:34)

Thus while the Deuteronomists made no attempt to
reassess the Mosaic covenant theology, but merely reiterated
it, and expressed the hope that the old covenant relationship
would after all be continued, Jeremiah 31 rejects the ancient

theology for an entirely new covenant 'not like the covenant which I made with their fathers'. His theology and that of the Deuteronomists are thus poles apart.[1] The Deuteronomic theology is rigidly pre-exilic, based solely on the arrangement entered into at Sinai and involving communal liability: Jeremiah's theology, by proclaiming that God is concerned with only one kind of liability, that of the individual, looks forward to the 'new covenant' theology evolved by Ezekiel, Deutero-Isaiah, and the Priestly theologians.

(iii)

EZEKIEL

Ezekiel, himself an exile, was the first theologian to come to terms with the fact that nothing now remained of the old order. The temple was destroyed and king, priests, and leading citizens were exiled in a heathen land. Unlike Hosea and the Deuteronomists, he no longer sees Israel's sojourn in the desert as an idyllic period in the past. Even in slavery in Egypt the Hebrews had rebelled against their God:

> On that day I swore to them that I would bring them out of the land of Egypt into a land that I had searched out for them, a land flowing with milk and honey, the most glorious of all lands. And I said to them, Cast away the detestable things your eyes feast on, every one of you, and do not defile yourselves with the idols of Egypt; I am the Lord your God. But they rebelled against me and would not listen to me; they did not every man cast away the detestable things their eyes feasted on, nor did they forsake the idols of Egypt.
> (20:6–8a)

---

[1] It is true that the Deuteronomic law recognized that only the person who actually committed an offence should be liable (Deut. 24: 16; cf. 2 Kings 9: 26). But this applied to the exercise of justice in Israelite courts. As far as God was concerned, the whole community remained liable for the offences of any member of that community (Deut. 5:9). Thus the Israelite courts reflected a greater understanding of justice than Israel's theology. The latter was tied to the Mosaic covenant concept, and it was only when judgment under that concept had taken place that a new theology could be proclaimed, in which God's standards were no longer held to be inferior to man's.

Indeed, at each stage of Israel's history God had every justification for terminating his relationship with her. That he had not done so was due to the foreign heathen nations who would wrongly interpret his act as weakness on his part in the face of their mightier gods:

> But I acted for the sake of my name, that it should not be profaned in the sight of the nations among whom they dwelt, in whose sight I made myself known to them in bringing them out of the land of Egypt.
>
> (20:9)

Graphically Ezekiel isolates the limitations of the pre-exilic covenant theology, based as it was on threat. For if God is to carry out his punishment of annihilating Israel, he will, putting it crudely, cut off his nose to spite his face. He is in fact in an insoluble dilemma. The defeat of Israel will be interpreted by the foreign nations as the defeat of Israel's God by their gods, and Israel's God will himself be left with no one to worship him.

But Israel's rebellion reached such proportions that in the end her God was left with no alternative. So judgment fell on Israel: God's relationship with her appeared to be at an end. But illogically Ezekiel proclaims that this is not to be the case. In spite of the long history of Israel's continued apostasy, God was not able to let her go. It was indeed in the exilic community itself, and not in those left in Jerusalem, that Israel's future was to be found. So God forsakes Jerusalem and goes to unclean Babylon (Ezek. 1). Ezekiel then recognized something about the essential nature of God which until then had not been properly grasped. Israel's God had indeed been too small. God could not do without man. So Ezekiel announces that God will bring about a second exodus:

> I will bring you out from the peoples and gather you out of the countries where you are scattered, with a mighty hand and an outstretched arm, and with wrath poured out.
>
> (20:34)

But this exodus will be radically different from the first exodus: there will be no new Sinai. In other words, no obligations will be laid on the restored community collectively. Instead, those individuals who accept God will be brought to their own land, and there form the new covenant community freed from the threat that should any member of that community fail to keep the law, the whole covenant relationship would be terminated. That Ezekiel was able to arrive at this new assessment of Israel's relationship with her God was due to his acceptance of the abolition of communal liability forecast by Jeremiah. Indeed he repeats the rejection of the popular proverb about sour grapes (18:1–4). The exiles saw themselves suffering for the sins of the previous generation. Ezekiel, while admitting that God had brought judgment under the pre-exilic theology for Israel's disobedience, holds that in spite of this anyone can still know God if only he will acknowledge him. It doesn't matter what his father has done; nor indeed what his former life has been:

> But if a wicked man turns away from all his sins which he has committed and keeps all my statutes and does what is lawful and right, he shall surely live; he shall not die. None of the transgressions which he has committed shall be remembered against him; for the righteousness which he has done he shall live. Have I any pleasure in the death of the wicked, says the Lord God, and not rather that he should turn from his way and live?
>
> (18:21–3)

But each individual had himself to accept God's offer of a direct personal relationship: he could not rely on others to achieve salvation for him. Thus Ezekiel rules out all possibility of vicarious salvation even by the most worthy heroes of the past:

> Son of man, when a land sins against me by acting faithlessly, and I stretch out my hand against it, and break its staff of bread and send famine upon it, and cut off from it man and beast, even if these three men, Noah, Daniel, and Job, were in it, they would deliver but their own lives by their righteousness, says the Lord God.
>
> (14:13–4)

Ezekiel's theology is, then, dominated by God's grace, and

this is beautifully brought out in the picture of the valley of dry bones:

> The hand of the Lord was upon me, and he brought me out by the Spirit of the Lord, and set me down in the midst of the valley; it was full of bones. And he led me round among them; and behold, there were very many upon the valley; and lo, they were very dry. And he said to me, 'Son of man, can these bones live?' And I answered, 'O Lord God, thou knowest.' Again he said to me, 'Prophesy to these bones, and say to them, O dry bones, hear the word of the Lord. Thus says the Lord God to these bones: Behold, I will cause breath to enter you, and you shall live. And I will lay sinews upon you, and will cause flesh to come upon you, and cover you with skin, and put breath in you, and you shall live; and you shall know that I am the Lord.'
>
> (37:1–6)

The image here is not that of resurrection but of re-creation. Israel is dead—like so many bones lying in a desert wadi after some bedouin skirmish, bones picked dry by the vultures and bleached white by the desert sun. The old order is at an end. There is a complete break. But then of his own free will God re-creates Israel and, as in the first creation (Gen. 2), he clothes the bones with flesh and breathes into them the breath of life. So a new Israel is born, an Israel who has done nothing, undertaken nothing, in return for her life, an Israel utterly dependent on God's grace for her existence.

Thus from the wreck of the Babylonian conquest Ezekiel not only proclaims a future but reveals to Israel the limitations of her existing theology, which in effect trapped God by his own threat of total judgment. But God is never trapped. He must because of his nature condemn utterly all that is opposed to his holiness, even his chosen people—but beyond God's judgment there is always a future. For God judges not to annihilate but to re-create. His anger is righteous and can only result in something positive. So when it came to the point, God could not let Israel go, nor would he ever do so. And through her cult, the restoration of which is vividly described by Ezekiel (40–48), her future was to be assured for all time. The Babylonian conquest had looked like the end:

it was in reality the beginning of a new and more wonderful relationship based on nothing else than divine love. It is not too much to say that it is Ezekiel rather than Ezra who deserves the title Father of Judaism. For it was through his theological insight that Israel found her future assured. He realized the nature of the God with whom not just Israel but all mankind has to deal. But, as Ezekiel impressed on the exiles, they had individually to appropriate that love, they had personally to stand on their own two feet. In spite of the evidence to the contrary, they had individually to show their faith in the God who would not, could not, let them go. Israel's future as the people of God was in their own hands. Man always determines his own fate, though God never exhausts his love.

(iv)

DEUTERO-ISAIAH

The generation to whom Ezekiel prophesied was to die in exile without seeing the fulfilment of his prophecy. Inevitably this led to considerable anxiety. Perhaps after all he had been a false prophet, perhaps Israel's relationship with her God had come to an end as pre-exilic theology said it would. So men, who against all the odds had remained faithful, began to question his activity. What was he doing on Israel's behalf? It was in answer to such questioning that an unknown prophet of the exile wrote. He has become known as Deutero-Isaiah because his words have been attached to the prophecy of Isaiah as Chapters 40–55. The prophet's answer is a triumphant vindication of Israel's God who even now was bringing into effect Israel's deliverance. Was it pure chance that the all-conquering Persian king Cyrus had appeared in the east to threaten Babylon?

> Who stirred up one from the east
> whom victory meets at every step?
> He gives up nations before him,
> so that he tramples kings under foot;
> he makes them like dust with his sword,
> like driven stubble with his bow.

He pursues them and passes on safely,
  by paths his feet have not trod.
Who has performed and done this,
  calling the generations from the beginning?
I, the Lord, the first,
  and with the last; I am He.

(41:2–4)

For those who had eyes to see, here was the hand of God
stretched out again to deliver his people from captivity.
Deutero-Isaiah thus confirms the prophecy of Ezekiel. The
new exodus foreseen by the earlier prophet is already dawning.
It will be quite different from the hasty flight from Egypt:
instead, it will be a triumphant march across a transformed
environment. Hills will be brought low and valleys exal-
ted to make a pleasant plain across which to march. And
the whole exercise will be in full view of the heathen nations who will have to draw their own conclusions about
the nature of Israel's God. As in Ezekiel, there will be no
need to stop at Sinai, for no obligations are to be imposed
on Israel. By God's grace and God's grace alone she
is to be restored to her own land in a relationship which
nothing now can break. Deutero-Isaiah confirms this rejection of the pre-exilic threat theology based on the Sinai
covenant by dramatically referring to Israel's three other
ancient covenant traditions—all covenants of promise without obligation: the covenants with Noah (Gen. 8:21–2),
Abraham (Gen. 17), and David (2 Sam. 7). So of Noah
he writes:

For this is like the days of Noah to me:
  as I swore that the waters of Noah
  should no more go over the earth,
so I have sworn that I will not be angry with you
  and will not rebuke you.
For the mountains may depart
  and the hills be removed,
but my steadfast love shall not depart from you,
  and my covenant of peace shall not be removed,
  says the Lord, who has compassion on you.

(54:9–10)

Nothing could be more explicit. Similarly, appeal is made to
the promise to Abraham:

> Look to Abraham your father
>   and to Sarah who bore you;
> for when he was but one I called him,
>   and I blessed him and made him many.
> For the Lord will comfort Zion;
>   he will comfort all her waste places,
> and will make her wilderness like Eden,
>   her desert like the garden of the Lord;
> joy and gladness will be found in her,
>   thanksgiving and the voice of song.
>
> (51:2–3)

But perhaps most significant of all is the use which Deutero-
Isaiah makes of the Davidic covenant tradition that David and
his heirs would rule Israel for ever. Instead of looking for the
restoration of the monarchy, Deutero-Isaiah transfers the
promise to David to the nation. This now becomes the everlasting people who will exist for all time come what may:

> Incline your ear, and come to me;
>   hear, that your soul may live;
> and I will make with you an everlasting covenant,
>   my steadfast, sure love for David.
>
> (55:3)

So for Deutero-Isaiah God is even now bringing about the
restoration of the elect people: the only doubt is whether the
exilic community will have sufficient faith to see his activity
in the events overtaking them, and so be able to claim his
everlasting promise that he will be their God and they will be
his people.

Deutero-Isaiah was the first Old Testament theologian
explicitly to enumerate the doctrine of monotheism—that
there *is* only one God. Previously Israel had worshipped only
one God, but had acknowledged the existence of other gods
with whom she was to have no dealings. No doubt the fact
that in Babylon the same claims were being made for the
Babylonian god Marduk as for Israel's God led Deutero-
Isaiah to make his far-reaching assertion. One of its immediate

consequences was that the nations of the world could no
longer be ignored. They must now have some relationship to
Israel's God who, since he was the only God, must have
created them. Thus Deutero-Isaiah proclaims Israel's role to
the world:

> I will give you as a light to the nations,
>> that my salvation may reach to the end of the earth.
>
> (49:6b)

The proclamation of the 'gospel' of God's grace—confirmed
by his action in delivering her from exile—is now to be
Israel's timeless mission to the world:

> Behold, you shall call nations that you know not,
>> and nations that knew you not shall run to you,
> because of the Lord your God, and of the Holy One
>> of Israel,
>> for he has glorified you.
>
> (55:5)

But in one respect Deutero-Isaiah's theology differs
markedly from Ezekiel's. He recognized that in the face of
widespread apostasy by his fellow Israelites in Babylon, and
the multitude of heathen nations to whom Israel now had a
responsibility, mankind's acceptance by God depended
ultimately on the faithfulness of a few. He thus reintroduced
the concept of vicarious salvation (53). It would be through
the sufferings of God's servant, most probably to be identified
as the righteous in Israel over against all Israel, that salvation
would be won for all mankind:

> By his knowledge shall the righteous one, my servant,
>> make many to be accounted righteous;
>> and he shall bear their iniquities.
> Therefore I will divide him a portion with the great,
>> and he shall divide the spoil with the strong;
> because he poured out his soul to death,
>> and was numbered with the transgressors:
> yet he bore the sin of many,
>> and made intercession for the transgressors.
>
> (53:11b–12)

So Deutero-Isaiah appealed to his fellow Israelites in exile, apparently forsaken by their God and of little consequence to their fellow men, to remain firm. It would be through their faithfulness in suffering that not only Israel would be restored, but the whole world would know the nature of the one gracious God with whom mankind has to deal.

Israel then has an atoning role to play. It was through her that God and man, all men, were to be at one. This is beautifully brought out in the metaphor of Israel as the priest-nation in Isa. 61:5–6, part of the post-exilic writings attached to Isaiah 1–55 and known by scholars as Trito-Isaiah:

> Aliens shall stand and feed your flocks,
>   foreigners shall be your ploughmen and vine-dressers;
> but you shall be called the priests of the Lord,
>   men shall speak of you as the ministers of our God;
> you shall eat the wealth of the nations,
>   and in their riches you shall glory.

Just as in ancient Israel the priests who were without any property secured their livelihood from the laity who tilled the land, so now Israel as the priest-nation to the world is to live off the foreign nations pictured as the laity doing all the manual work. But Israel is not simply to luxuriate in her rich idleness: she has a specific task. As the priest-nation she is to mediate God's blessing to the world. The same idea is present in Zech. 8:23:

> Thus says the Lord of hosts: In those days ten men from the nations of every tongue shall take hold of the robe of a Jew, saying, 'Let us go with you, for we have heard that God is with you.'

It is through each individual Jew, himself a priest to the world, that all the world will be brought into relationship with the one God. For post-exilic Israel, then, the world was her parish, for it was God's world, and all men part of his creation to be brought within the elect community which ultimately is mankind itself.

(v)

THE PRIESTLY WORK

But what of the law? Where did this fit into the new covenant of sheer grace enunciated by Ezekiel and Deutero-Isaiah? If Israel was no longer under threat of judgment, was it all superfluous? On the contrary, the law became not the instrument of judgment, but the means of grace. Here we come to the Priestly Work, the reinterpretation of the ancient literary accounts of Israel's origins by the Priestly theologians which resulted in the Tetrateuch, Genesis–Numbers. Like Ezekiel and Deutero-Isaiah, the Priestly theologians are no longer primarily concerned with the covenant at Sinai. For them, Israel's history is determined by her divine election— an election which took place at the very creation of the world and which nothing now can cancel. This is brought out by the Priestly theologians in the very first chapter of their Work and explains why a second creation account had to be written (Gen. 1–2:4a). Taking over an eight-day Babylonian creation story, they compressed it into six days, so that on the seventh day they could record the inauguration of the sabbath. In other words, the sabbath was shown to be as fixed in the very scheme of things as sun and moon, sea and land, animals and men. And since the only people in the world who kept the sabbath were the Jews, they too were fixed in God's creation: their election was assured for all time. Indeed, for the Priestly theologians the events of Sinai are not seen as the inauguration of a new relationship between God and the Hebrew slaves, but merely as the fulfilment of the promise to Abraham. Whereas under the Sinai covenant God's relationship with Israel was conditional on obedience to the law, the Priestly writers saw that that relationship existed prior to the giving of that law, and therefore was independent of it. They recognized that failure was inherent in man and that the cult, with above all its Day of Atonement (Lev. 16), provided the means whereby Israel might ever renew and reform herself, and so be the people whom God desired her to be. The Priestly legislation was therefore designed to ensure the proper ordering of cult and people. It recognized that some people would have to be excluded, for only those who were in a fit state could come into God's presence. Certain acts would take one outside the community for ever. The law therefore protected the existing and permanent relationship of God and Israel from abuse. But it did not create that relationship, nor did it determine its duration. The 'new covenant' of Jeremiah was for ever. While those who failed to measure up to God's standards would find themselves excluded, Israel herself would never again be rejected.

Thus the importance of law in post-exilic Israel was in no way diminished for the individual Israelite. It determined his membership of the elect community. If he did not obey the law, then he could not consider himself part of that community. There were rules, and to break the rules—certainly in any fundamental way—would mean exclusion from the community for all time.[1] But the community itself was not affected, as it would have been prior to the exile, by the disobedience of any individual member. This was the totally new situation following the return from exile. Israel—now no longer a national political entity, but rather a worshipping community centred on the rebuilt temple at Jerusalem—would continue to exist come what may, so long as there remained one person who still kept the law.

For pre-exilic threat theology (eighth-century prophets and Deuteronomy) God of his grace directly entered into a relationship with Israel, obedience to the law determining the existence of that relationship. In other words the law came between God and Israel. But in the post-exilic theology of sheer grace (Ezekiel, Deutero-Isaiah, and the Priestly theologians) nothing came between God and his people. Their relationship depended solely on his grace and would in consequence exist for all time. Nothing could invalidate Israel's election. For the law's function was not to determine whether or not the covenant relationship was to be maintained, but simply to decide who individually made up the elect community. Further, anyone could become a member of that

---

[1] Apart from murder, for which the death penalty continued to be exacted, excommunication from the elect community became the recognized post-exilic punishment for crime.

community irrespective of previous race, colour, or religion, if he simply agreed to obey that law. The invitation to election was open to all. All these relationships can best be illustrated by a further diagram:

Pre-exilic theology **Post-exilic theology**

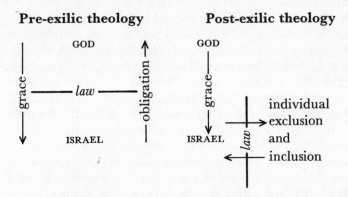

We can, then, now isolate the gospel of the Old Testament. It is the triumphant assertion that God's grace triumphs over his law—that man and God are ever to be in communion. This is indeed *good news*.

But there is one further aspect of ancient Israel's understanding of her God that needs examining. Though it is clear that God wills man to be in relationship with him, it is also clear that man remains part of the created order and so dependent on him. This being so, in what sense can man know God? Are there in fact necessary limitations to the kind of belief which he can have? To these problems we must now turn.

3

The Absent God

Alongside the priest and the prophet, ancient Israel had a third professional class known as the wise (Jer. 18:18), who by their advice sought to achieve an ordered existence both for society at large and individuals personally. The wise recognized that God had created the world out of chaos and established a divine order. It was their task from their observation of the world around them to fit man into it. Wisdom was thus anthropomorphic rather than theocentric in that it necessarily approached the problem of life from man's standpoint as he experienced it. But this does not mean that it was therefore secular. For even when it was dealing with everyday activity, it was seeking to relate that activity to the divine order which God had established and in which man must live out his life. The counsel of the wise therefore concerned every facet of public and private life. Their particular aptitude lay in their ability to see the order in things, how one thing related to another, how society functioned, how the natural world and science worked. The wise looked at relationships, objects, and ideas, and tried to discern their pattern, their structure, and order. Their concern was that men should be able to live the best and fullest lives, and not come to any mishap. Above all, the wise man was expected to be able so to manipulate words that order might either be maintained or restored. He was the man who knew what to say in an awkward situation, and by saying it brought about peace and harmony. The most famous example of this, and one which well illustrates the function of the wise, is Solomon's judgment in the case of the two prostitutes and one surviving child (1 Kings 3). Here was a situation which seemed impossible of solution. Yet Solomon by his wise words was able to bring order out of chaos and restore the child to its rightful mother.

Wisdom, then, complemented law, for like law it sought to achieve and maintain that divine order which God had inaugurated at creation but which was ever threatened by man's folly, his predilection for disorderly conduct. So Adam disobeys God's rules for tilling Eden, and chaos enters God's creation. Thus we find in the wisdom literature the same concern for dependent members of society which we saw in the law and the prophets:

> Do not say to your neighbour, 'Go, and come again,
>   tomorrow I will give it'—when you have it with you.
> (Prov. 3:28)

> Do not rob the poor, because he is poor,
>   or crush the afflicted at the gate.
> (Prov. 22:22)

> Do not remove an ancient landmark
>   or enter the fields of the fatherless.
> (Prov. 23:10)

Further, this literature echoes the prophetic protest in its rejection of the outward forms of religion if these are not accompanied by right actions towards one's neighbour:

> To do righteousness and justice
>   is more acceptable to the Lord than sacrifice.
> (Prov. 21:3)

> If one turns away his ear from hearing the law,
>   even his prayer is an abomination.
> (Prov. 28:9)

But while early wisdom literature did not question the moral order of the world, later post-exilic wisdom literature, of which Job, Proverbs, and Ecclesiastes all form part, was almost entirely preoccupied with the question of whether man got his just deserts. For with the post-exilic concentration on the individual as opposed to the community at large, it came to be increasingly recognized that disaster fell on the good as on the bad, and the wicked prospered with the righteous.

How then could orthodox theology continue to maintain that there was a moral order in the world for which God was responsible?

Proverbs takes a largely optimistic view of life, believing that through a combination of diligent searching and discipline man can in fact discover the moral order in the world, and so find complete fulfilment to his life:

> Happy is the man who finds wisdom,
>   and the man who gets understanding,
> for the gain from it is better than gain from silver
>   and its profit better than gold.
> She is more precious than jewels,
>   and nothing you desire can compare with her.
> Long life is in her right hand;
>   in her left hand are riches and honour.
> Her ways are ways of pleasantness,
>   and all her paths are peace.
> She is a tree of life to those who lay hold of her;
>   those who hold her fast are called happy.
>
> (3:13-18)

Proverbs unquestioningly accepts the orthodox doctrine of rewards, that is, that it is the guilty who suffer, while the righteous are blessed:

> A good man obtains favour from the Lord,
>   but a man of evil devices he condemns.
>
> (12:2)

> No ill befalls the righteous,
>   but the wicked are filled with trouble.
>
> (12:21)

> Honour the Lord with your substance
>   and with the firstfruits of all your produce;
> then your barns will be filled with plenty,
>   and your vats will be bursting with wine.
>
> (3:9-10)

Indeed, such is the author's faith that he confidently counsels men against taking the law into their own hands. God himself will act as the avenger:

> Do not say, 'I will repay evil';
> wait for the Lord, and he will help you.
>
> (20:22)

Man can indeed place his whole trust in God:

> Many seek the favour of a ruler,
> but from the Lord a man gets justice.
>
> (29:26)

Against this background, Proverbs works out what amounts to a code of conduct to cover every contingency of life which goes far beyond the law codes. But its goal is the same, for through obedience the righteous will inevitably enjoy fullness of life:

> He who gives heed to the word will prosper,
> and happy is he who trusts in the Lord.
>
> (16:20)

Ecclesiastes, on the other hand, boldly recognizes that the facts of life do not always measure up to orthodox theological claims. Its conclusion is therefore decidedly pessimistic:

> I have seen everything that is done under the sun; and behold, all is vanity and a striving after wind.
>
> (1:14)

In considering the respective fortunes of the living and the dead, the author recognizes that there is in fact a third class of people even better off—the unborn:

> And I thought the dead who are already dead more fortunate than the living who are still alive; but better than both is he who has not yet been, and has not seen the evil deeds that are done under the sun.
>
> (4:2–3)

The author concludes that life is utterly capricious, and the wisest course open to man is to try and be on good terms with God, keep his commandments, and hope for the best. There is nothing one can do to insure against the possibility of disaster, for there is in fact no moral order in the world:

> There is a vanity which takes place on earth, that there are righteous men to whom it happens according to the deeds of

the wicked, and there are wicked men to whom it happens
according to the deeds of the righteous. I said that this also is
vanity. And I commend enjoyment, for man has no good
thing under the sun but to eat, and drink, and enjoy himself,
for this will go with him in his toil through the days of life
which God gives him under the sun.

$$(8:14-15)$$

Again I saw that under the sun the race is not to the swift,
nor the battle to the strong, nor bread to the wise, nor riches
to the intelligent, nor favour to the men of skill; but time and
chance happen to them all. For man does not know his
time. Like fish which are taken in an evil net, and like birds
which are caught in a snare, so the sons of men are snared at
an evil time, when it suddenly falls upon them.

$$(9:11-12)$$

But where between these two extremes lies Job? The book
consists of a Prologue (1–2) and Epilogue (42:7ff.), originally
part of a much older tale, into which has been inserted the
Dialogue between Job and his friends (3–27, 29–31), a
wisdom poem (28), the speeches of Elihu (32–7), and the reply
of God (38–42:6).

The Prologue pictures Job as an entirely righteous man,
innocent of all sin, who in consequence enjoys the fullness of
God's blessing in the material riches of his life.[1] The Satan,
who is in no way to be thought of as the devil of later
theology but as a more than averagely intelligent member of
the divine court, asks God some awkward questions about
man and his relationship with God. He argues that if Job
were to lose his possessions, or worse still, to be physically
afflicted, his piety would soon evaporate. He knows Job to
be innocent of any offence and does not accuse him of hidden
wrongs, but he believes that his faith cannot be disinterested.
God gives consent to a test.

Faced with this appalling situation involving a total
reversal of his fortune, Job might well have given up. This is
what his wife advises him to do. Seeing the hopelessness of his
position, she deduces that there is no point in his prolonging

---

[1] Eccles. 7:20 avoids this problem by saying that no such man as Job could
exist. Consequently it never reaches the insight of Job.

his life. So she advises him to curse God and die—that is to commit suicide, for God would automatically strike the blasphemer dead. But Job tells her that she speaks like one of the foolish women. She cannot even discern that life of necessity has its ups and downs. Having experienced the goodness of God, it is simply illogical to renounce him now when things have gone wrong. So Job remains firm and passes Satan's test as to whether or not his religion is disinterested in the Prologue itself. But a very different Job appears in the Dialogue, a Job who is anything but submissive to his lot:

> After this Job opened his mouth and cursed the day of his birth. And Job said:
> 'Let the day perish wherein I was born,
>   and the night which said,
>   "A man-child is conceived."
> Let that day be darkness!
>   May God above not seek it,
>   nor light shine upon it.
> Let gloom and deep darkness claim it.
>   Let clouds dwell upon it;
>   let the blackness of the day terrify it.'

$$(3:1-5)$$

It is this entirely different picture of Job presented by the Dialogue which led Charles Williams[1] to write of the author:

> His work has saved Christendom from being misled by Saint Paul's rash refusal to allow the thing formed to ask questions of him that formed it, the pot of the potter: one of those metaphors which miss the bull while thudding the target. . . . No pot—so far—has asked questions of the potter in a voice the potter can understand; when it does, it will be time enough to compare pots to me. The criticism is not aimed at Saint Paul who dropped the phrase in the midst of a great spiritual wrestle, not as a moral instruction. But it has been used too often by the pious to encourage them to say, in love or in laziness, 'Our little minds were never meant. . . .' Fortunately there is the book of Job to make it clear that our little minds were meant. A great curiosity ought to exist concerning divine things. Man was intended to argue with God.

[1] *He Came Down from Heaven*, London, 1950, pp. 29f.

To understand the Dialogue between Job and his three friends, it is necessary to recognize its literary form. It is in fact couched as a lawsuit in which Job is seen as the plaintiff challenging traditional theology and the three friends constitute the defendants of Jewish orthodoxy. So Ludwig Köhler[1] has shown that there is in fact little connection between the speeches of the two parties, which invariably begin with rhetorical abuse typical of law court technique. Such is Bildad's complaint, that Job speaks for a long time but that his argument lacks any content:

> How long will you say these things,
>   and the words of your mouth be a great wind?
>
> (8:2)

Such also is Job's mockery of the friends:

> No doubt you are the people,
>   and wisdom will die with you.
> But I have understanding as well as you;
>   I am not inferior to you.
> Who does not know such things as these?
>
> (12:2–3)

and Eliphaz's charge that Job's case lacks substance:

> Should a wise man answer with windy knowledge,
>   and fill himself with the east wind?
> Should he argue in unprofitable talk,
>   or in words with which he can do no good?
>
> (15:2–3)

This is, then, no Platonic dialogue in which the argument proceeds to an unknown point. Rather each side has adopted a rigidly determined position and seeks to silence the other by the force of his case. So we need not look for progression as the case unfolds, but rather can examine the briefs of the two parties independently.

But what is the substance of the action? Merely from the Prologue it seems to be the possibility of disinterested religion in the face of innocent suffering, which in the case of Job

---

[1] *Hebrew Man*, London, 1956, pp. 158ff.

includes both moral and non-moral evil. But that issue has
already been settled by Job's reply to his wife. He is not so
stupid as to acknowledge God only when things go right for
him. His faith is genuine. But the Dialogue uses the problem
of unjust suffering as the framework for a much wider question, that is the nature of the relationship between man and
God. It asks the fundamental question: what kind of a belief
can man have? Job's faith is no longer at issue: his persistent
arguing confirms it. Rather it is orthodox Jewish religion—a
religion which claims to have all the answers—which finds
itself on trial.

But before examining the cases of the parties, it is important to recognize that the possibility of a future life in which
this world's wrongs will be righted does not enter into the
discussion. The most that the Hebrew can hope for is, as
Eliphaz says, that

> You shall come to your grave in ripe old age,
>   as a shock of grain comes up to the threshing floor in its
>   season.
>
> (5:26)

This is the reward that Job receives in the Epilogue:

> And after this Job lived a hundred and forty years, and saw
> his sons, and his sons' sons, four generations. And Job died,
> an old man, and full of days.
>
> (42:16–17)

For the Hebrew, life was carried on in his descendants. It
was his name—that is, his personality—that lived on, while
he descended to the shadowy life of Sheol, where he existed
in a kind of permanent limbo. It is true that he could be
spirited up through necromancy (1 Sam. 28:11ff.) but this
was strictly forbidden and highly irregular. Unfortunately
Handel's use of 'I know that my Redeemer liveth' has
induced a good many people to believe that Job 19:25 refers
to life after death. But whatever this verse means, and the
Hebrew is notoriously difficult, it must be judged by the
general context of the book, which remains strictly orthodox
on the doctrine of Sheol and the afterlife:

As the cloud fades and vanishes,
   so he who goes down to Sheol does not come up;
he returns no more to his house,
   nor does his place know him any more.

(7:9–10)

For there is hope for a tree,
   if it be cut down, that it will sprout again,
   and that its shoots will not cease.
Though its root grow old in the earth,
   and its stump die in the ground,
yet at the scent of water it will bud
   and put forth branches like a young plant.
But man dies, and is laid low;
   man breathes his last, and where is he?
As waters fail from a lake,
   and a river wastes away and dries up,
So man lies down and rises not again;
   till the heavens are no more he will not awake,
   or be roused out of his sleep.
Oh that thou wouldest hide me in Sheol,
   that thou wouldest conceal me until thy wrath be past,
   that thou wouldest appoint me a set time, and remember me!
If a man die, shall he live again?
   All the days of my service I would wait,
   till my release should come.

(14:7–14)

The whole point of the last two verses is that they envisage something that is totally impossible. The most we may say of Job 19:25 is that somehow after his death Job will be brought from Sheol and witness his vindication at the hands of his personal representative.

But in any event, life after death does not solve the problem of innocent suffering in this world, nor does it help to answer the basic question of the nature of the God–man relationship. Christians believe, as the Hebrews believed, because they know God now, not because they shall know him hereafter. They may have good reason to suppose that this life is not the end, but that supposition does not account for their faith here and now. Christianity, like Judaism, is not a religion of rewards hereafter, but a present relationship with the living

God. It is the nature of this relationship that is Job's concern.

Job opens his case by asking why man was created at all. He cannot 'curse God and die' for God is a living reality to him. So he curses the day of his birth for, as we shall see, bringing him to this conflict between on the one hand his experience of life and on the other his experience of God. For him life has become utterly meaningless and pointless. His position on the dung-heap covered in sores, an outcast of the city, serves to heighten this. Job realizes that all there is left for him is Sheol. Why not get the mockery of living over at once and descend there, where at least there are no rewards, no punishments, and no illusions:

> There the wicked cease from troubling,
>   and there the weary are at rest.
> There the prisoners are at ease together;
>   they hear not the voice of the taskmaster.
> The small and the great are there,
>   and the slave is free from his master.

> (3:17–19)

For Job life no longer seems to be controlled by any moral order. He knows himself to be innocent, yet God has dreadfully afflicted him. Life has become a cruel game in which all the rules appear to have been abandoned in God's favour. Worse still, God doesn't seem to care enough even to offer an explanation of what has happened. So Job pleads that God would himself enter into the lawsuit. Why doesn't he take the witness-stand and answer Job's charge? For all the evidence indicates that it is God who has acted immorally:

> Oh, that I knew where I might find him,
>   that I might come even to his seat!
> I would lay my case before him
>   and fill my mouth with arguments.
> I would learn what he would answer me,
>   and understand what he would say to me.
> Would he contend with me in the greatness of his power?
>   No; he would give heed to me.
> There an upright man could reason with him,
>   and I should be acquitted for ever by my judge.

> (23:3–7)

But earlier in his case Job had despairingly concluded that even if God did appear, justice would still not be done:

> If it is a contest of strength, behold him!
>> If it is a matter of justice, who can summon him?
> Though I am innocent, my own mouth would condemn me;
>> though I am blameless, he would prove me perverse.
> I am blameless; I regard not myself;
>> I loathe my life.
> It is all one; therefore I say,
>> he destroys both the blameless and the wicked.
> When disaster brings sudden death,
>> he mocks at the calamity of the innocent.
> The earth is given into the hand of the wicked;
>> he covers the faces of its judges—

And then almost as if he cannot really believe what he has said, Job adds:

> if it is not he, who then is it?

$$(9:19-24)$$

Desperately Job implores God to allow there to be the same sort of justice between God and man as can be obtained in earthly courts between men:

> My friends scorn me;
>> my eye pours out tears to God,
> that he would maintain the right of a man with God,
>> like that of a man with his neighbour.

$$(16:20-1)$$

But look at the wicked:

> Why do the wicked live,
>> reach old age, and grow mighty in power?
>
> They spend their days in prosperity,
>> and in peace they go down to Sheol.
> They say to God, 'Depart from us!
>> We do not desire the knowledge of thy ways.
> What is the Almighty, that we should serve him?
>> And what profit do we get if we pray to him?'
> Behold, is not their prosperity in their hand?

$$(21:7, 13-16a)$$

The orthodox reply is that if the wicked don't get punished, then their sons will, but Job replies that once they are in Sheol that will hardly concern them. Let them be afflicted now:

> You say, 'God stores up their iniquity for their sons.'
>   Let him recompense it to themselves, that they may know it.
> Let their own eyes see their destruction,
>   and let them drink of the wrath of the Almighty.
> For what do they care for their houses after them,
>   when the number of their months is cut off?
>
> (21:19–21)

Indeed Job, as he looks out on the mass of human misery which disfigures the world, can only conclude that God has forsaken the just and those who cry to him for help. There is no hope for mankind with him:

> Why are not times of judgment kept by the Almighty,
>   and why do those who know him never see his days?
>
> From out of the city the dying groan,
>   and the soul of the wounded cries for help;'
> yet God pays no attention to their prayer.
>
> (24:1, 12)

But Job need not have worried about God's possible appearance, for God makes no attempt to take the witness stand. He remains totally silent. Job is utterly alone—no one understands him, no one believes in him, neither wife nor friends, and God has denied him his presence. In this absolute position of isolation Job is forced to make the all-or-nothing decision. Will he remain true not only to the God whom he has known and whose favour he has enjoyed, but also to his own integrity—or will he deny one or the other? Job is brought to the test. And in that test he has to act alone, relying on nothing but his own experience and what he can deduce from it.

The temptation for Job is clear enough—to come down on one side or the other, to deny God or his own innocence. Ironically, Eliphaz had recognized at the beginning of the trial that it was faith in God and the integrity of the individual believer that was at issue:

> Is not your fear of God your confidence,
>   and the integrity of your ways your hope?
>
> (4:6)

But there is only one way open to Job whereby he can affirm his innocence and yet also proclaim his trust in God. This is through the curse-formula, for the Hebrews believed that divine action must follow every curse. So Job curses not God but himself, and thereby forces God's hand. He does this by listing every conceivable wrong which a man might have committed and for which it might be thought that God was punishing him. The long list of possible offences is set out in Job 31, of which the following form examples:

> If I have withheld anything that the poor desired,
>   or have caused the eyes of the widow to fail,
> or have eaten my morsel alone,
>   and the fatherless has not eaten of it;
>
> if I have seen any one perish for lack of clothing,
>   or a poor man without covering;
>
> If I have made gold my trust,
>   or called fine gold my confidence;
>
> If I have rejoiced at the ruin of him that hated me,
>   or exulted when evil overtook him.
>
> (31:16–17, 19, 24, 29)

If God can show that Job is guilty of any of these charges, then Job will accept his punishment without complaint, for he will no longer be the innocent sufferer. But by listing the offences in the curse-formula, Job makes it impossible for God to remain silent, for a curse was a direct challenge to God, which he was unable to ignore. God must now appear and answer Job; he must either condemn or acquit him of the all-embracing list of offences. He must in effect disclose why Job is suffering. The lawsuit must have a verdict. As the great Old Testament scholar Wheeler Robinson has written:

'This is an appeal to God against God with the daring illogicality of faith.'[1] Job to the last has kept his integrity:

> As God lives, who has taken away my right,
>   and the Almighty, who has made my soul bitter;
> as long as my breath is in me,
>   and the spirit of God is in my nostrils;
> my lips will not speak falsehood,
>   and my tongue will not utter deceit.
> Far be it from me to say that you [the friends] are right;
>   till I die I will not put away my integrity from me.
> I hold fast my righteousness, and will not let it go;
>   my heart does not reproach me for any of my days.
>
> (27:2-6)

Entering into the fullness of the dark abyss, the silent unknown, Job is forced in the agony of the absent God to make the all-or-nothing decision: to commit suicide or to express faith. Despised and rejected, he triumphantly makes the assertion 'In spite of . . . , I believe', and in consequence knows again God's presence.

The three friends seek to defend God from Job's charge. It is incorrect to attempt to distinguish their views for they present essentially the same arguments. Indeed their differentiation as persons is simply due to the borrowed Prologue where the friends are named. Their case is based on the orthodox standpoint that suffering was the result of sin. So Eliphaz says:

> Think now, who that was innocent ever perished?
>   Or where were the upright cut off?
>
> (4:7)

One must trust God:

> As for me, I would seek God,
>   and to God would I commit my cause.
>
> (5:8)

Eliphaz even goes so far as to counsel Job to rejoice in his suffering:

> Behold, happy is the man whom God reproves;
>   therefore despise not the chastening of the Almighty.

[1] H. Wheeler Robinson, *The Cross in the Old Testament*, London, 1955, p. 30.

For he wounds, but he binds up;
  he smites, but his hands heal.

(5:17–18)

At one point his argument becomes entirely fatalistic:

But man is born to trouble
  as the sparks fly upward.

(5:7)

But as defenders of the faith, the friends cannot accept the
legitimacy of Job's plea of innocence:

Does God pervert justice?
  Or does the Almighty pervert the right?
If your children have sinned against him,
  he has delivered them into the power of their transgression.
If you will seek God
  and make supplication to the Almighty,
if you are pure and upright,
  surely then he will rouse himself for you
  and reward you with a rightful habitation.
And though your beginning was small,
  your latter days will be very great.

(8:3–7)

For the three friends Job's case should never have been
brought. God is unknowable save in what he chooses to
disclose. Job as a mere man cannot understand him and it is
presumptuous of him to try:

Can you find out the deep things of God?
  Can you find out the limit of the Almighty?

(11:7)

Are you the first man that was born?
  Or were you brought forth before the hills?
Have you listened in the council of God?
  And do you limit wisdom to yourself?

(15:7–8)

But while speaking entirely appropriately of the transcendence of God, the friends never attempt to help Job reconcile

his own belief in God with the unjustness of his suffering, but deny both. Job is faithless and deserves to be condemned. It is easier to brand the questioner a heretic and unrighteous than to face up to the fact that one's theology may be deficient:

> Why does your heart carry you away,
>   and why do your eyes flash,
> that you turn your spirit against God,
>   and let such words go out of your mouth?
> What is man, that he can be clean?
>   Or he that is born of a woman, that he can be righteous?
> Behold, God puts no trust in his holy ones,
>   and the heavens are not clean in his sight;
> how much less one who is abominable and corrupt,
>   a man who drinks iniquity like water!
>
> (15:12–16)

Frightened that their theological presuppositions might be upset by the questionings of this wretched fellow, the friends fall back on the stock answers of their creed. It is quite correct to say that God cannot be the subject of a legal suit, but this will hardly comfort the innocent sufferer driven to ask 'Why?' And this is no improper question, for as the book of Job points out, one may not get the answer, but to argue with God will not destroy faith nor produce an irrational faith, but will test faith and so deepen one's relationship with him.

In what way does Job's position differ from that of the friends? Fundamentally they agree on the transcendence of God and cannot explain unjust suffering. But while the friends are content to repeat the orthodox view that since God is good, it must be Job who is guilty and so deserves suffering, Job knows that this is untrue and submits himself utterly to God, denying neither God's justness nor his own innocence. But Job's question remains. Why are the innocent afflicted with the guilty? If God does not do this, who does? Job, in his direct appeal to God through the self-curse, makes the great assertion of faith: 'In spite of . . . , I believe,' while the friends, under the protective cover of orthodox theology, seek to avoid the reality of the issue. But for Job, the innocent sufferer, the issue cannot be avoided. If God is the person he supposed him to be, how could he be the author of such suffering?

After the rigours of the Dialogue there follow the speeches of the young Elihu. These have probably been inserted because a later generation felt it improper that the omnipotent and transcendent God should immediately obey Job's summons—though the use of the curse-formula dictated this. In fact the speeches add little to the case save that Elihu tries to justify suffering by the discipline it can bring. But there is much suffering in the world which cannot be covered in this way—suffering leading to lunacy, for instance. While we can use suffering for a positive purpose once it has arisen, this does not explain why it should have to occur in the first place.

Then the reader gets what he has been waiting for—the judgment of God. From the book's beginning he has known that God must answer Job's indictment, the trial must have a verdict. But the surprise of God's judgment is that far from simply vindicating Job, whom the reader knows all along to be innocent, God, in very much the same language as the three friends (cf. 11:7ff.; 15:7ff.), proclaims his utter transcendence and confirms that man cannot know as God knows. The wish to do so was the basic sin of Eden. The tension which Job has discovered is to be maintained not dissipated. But notwithstanding this, Job is nowhere condemned for questioning God. Though in the face of God's personal appearance before him, Job acknowledges that he cannot know as God knows, yet God specifically rewards him for what he has *said*:

> After the Lord had spoken these words to Job, the Lord said to Eliphaz the Temanite: 'My wrath is kindled against you and against your two friends; for you have not spoken of me what is right, *as my servant Job has*.'
>
> (42:7)

Job has been right to reject the false answers of the friends, even though they were sanctioned by orthodox theology; he has been right to argue with God, to force him to appear; his only error lay in the assumption that when he did appear everything would be made plain.[1] Instead, God, in coming to Job in his total isolation, confirms that he remains God and Job remains man. But by coming, God shows that he stands with Job in the fullness of his misery though he does not explain why Job should have to endure it. He is in effect told that the belief 'in spite of' is all man can have on earth. This is the nature of the God–man relationship. In risking all through his self-curse, Job discovers the necessity of an agnostic faith.

On the other hand the three friends are condemned. Why this was so in the ancient story taken over in the Prologue and Epilogue is not known. Perhaps they agreed with the wife. But now they are condemned because, while they rested their case on the proper doctrine of the transcendence of God, they failed to enter into the reality of Job's experience, but denied it. So, ironically, those who relied on orthodox theology had in the end to depend on 'the heretic' Job for their acceptance by God:

> Now therefore take seven bulls and seven rams, and go to my servant Job, and offer up for yourselves a burnt offering; and my servant Job shall pray for you, for I will accept his prayer not to deal with you according to your folly; for you have not spoken of me what is right, as my servant Job has.
>
> (42:8)

The conclusion to the book, which is as appropriate for the author of the Dialogue as for the author of the original story

---

[1] It has sometimes been argued that Job is rewarded by God only because he repents of his presumption in arguing with him. But quite apart from such a conclusion making nonsense of the book—it is through Job's argument that a proper theology evolves—doubt has now been thrown on the usual translation of Job 42:6, given in the RSV as:

therefore I despise myself,
and repent in dust and ashes.

In a recent note in the Old Testament journal, *Vetus Testamentum* (xxvi, 1976, pp. 369–71), Dale Patrick argues that the verse should be rendered:

therefore I repudiate and repent
of dust and ashes.

In other words Job 42:1–6 is to be understood as a paean of praise at God's disclosure to Job of his might, which enables Job to abandon his position of mourning among the dust and ashes assumed in Job 2:8.

partly presented in the Prologue, is a fairy-tale ending in accord with the beliefs of the times. Job receives the maximum reward that man can have on earth and can go peacefully to Sheol:

> And the Lord blessed the latter days of Job more than his beginning; and he had fourteen thousand sheep, six thousand camels, a thousand yoke of oxen, and a thousand she-asses. He had also seven sons and three daughters. . . . And after this Job lived a hundred and forty years, and saw his sons, and his sons' sons, four generations. And Job died, an old man, and full of days.
>
> (42:12–13, 16–17)

So while the Prologue concerned the man who meekly accepts suffering, showing that disinterested religion is possible, the Dialogue pictures a very different situation, the man who neither accepts unjust suffering nor rejects God. Job, like Jacob at the Jabbok (Gen. 32:22–32), wrestles with God and will not let him go until he has answered him. God is able to answer him because Job has remained true not only to God, but also to himself. This is what God wants of men.

But the book gives no answer to the problem of suffering. Indeed God never even mentions it. He properly points out his might, majesty, dominion, and power—and leaves it like that. Wheeler Robinson therefore felt able to argue from the Prologue that the origin of suffering must lie at God's door. He believed that while we cannot understand it, we can know that it is part of the will of God, and so can respond to God's trust in us by the practice of disinterested religion. This is our cross.[1]

But after the Dialogue, is it any longer possible to take seriously the details of the Prologue, to base one's theology in the consent of God to Satan's test? For the whole point of the Dialogue is that it is thoroughly agnostic about the origin of suffering. The author doesn't know and so cannot answer why men suffer unjustly. And men must be content to leave it like that. What he does say, though, is that in spite of this suffering, man can still know God and be in relationship with him: that

[1] Wheeler Robinson, *The Cross in the Old Testament*, pp. 42ff.

is, not even suffering can separate us from the love of God, a point which Paul makes very clear in the Epistle to the Romans:

> For I am sure that neither death, nor life, nor angels, nor principalities, nor things present, nor things to come, nor powers, nor height, nor depth, nor anything else in all creation, will be able to separate us from the love of God in Christ Jesus our Lord.
>
> (8:38–9)

All the Prologue does, then, is to explain how a certain situation arose—Job's wretched state. But while it reserves for God his ultimate omnipotence in that he is made to give consent to Satan's experiment, it is not intended as a theological explanation of the origin of evil. Exactly the same is true of the story of Adam's disobedience, which incidentally—like the Prologue of Job—has no subsequent influence on the story. Its aim is simply to describe man's state of separation from God, from which God proceeds to rescue him. But in attributing the original temptation to the serpent, part of the created order, the author does not intend to tell us anything theological about the origin of evil or God's part in it.

The book of Job thus indicates that man cannot have an explanation of everything: whether he likes it or not, he must over some things remain agnostic, though he can be an agnostic believer. Indeed, Job tells us much more about man than about God, for God remains transcendent throughout, never disclosing his secrets, but to the end throwing back that wretched 'why?' that humanity has cried since the dawn of time. But man, in his ability to say 'I believe', is every bit as much a mystery as God. Ironically, with the Psalmist, Job asks:

> What is man, that thou dost make so much of him,
> and that thou dost set thy mind upon him,
> dost visit him every morning,
> and test him every moment?
>
> (7:17–18)

But as we have already seen, it was ancient Israel's particular

insight to recognize that man was as necessary to God as God
was to man. So Job is not afraid to remind God that should
anything happen to Job, it would be he, God, who would be
every bit as much the loser:

> Why dost thou not pardon my transgression
>   and take away my iniquity?
> For now I shall lie in the earth;
>   thou wilt seek me, but I shall not be.
>
> (7:21)

Thus oddly enough, in contrast to the facile optimism of
the book of Proverbs, the conclusion of Job is very similar to
that of Ecclesiastes. Life is unfair, men do suffer unjustly,
there is apparently no moral order—but in spite of all this one
can know God. For Ecclesiastes this is a pessimistic conclusion, but for Job optimistic, for Job recognizes that this
knowledge of God is the one thing that matters for the wise
man. This is summed up very neatly in Chapter 28, itself a
late addition to the book. Here, against the simile of mining
for precious metal, and in total contradiction to Proverbs
2:1–5, wisdom is presented as being quite beyond man's
discovery: only God knows the way to it. Wisdom belongs to
him alone: he alone has all the answers. Yet God chooses to
enter into relationship with man, he chooses to disclose
himself to man. This is the meaning of the closing couplet of
the poem:

> Behold, the fear of the Lord, that is wisdom;
>   and to depart from evil is understanding.
>
> (28:28)

It is through man's religion, his relationship with God—for
that is what 'fear of the Lord' means—that man will find that
order, peace, and harmony which he seeks, and which he
cannot experience otherwise from this disordered world. But
how that disorder arose, the book of Job does nothing to
explain.

Of all the wisdom literature Job, then, is the most profound,
for the author brings home to man what must be the nature
of his belief. For although Job ends up in the same position as
the three friends, unable to place God in the dock, he knows,

as the friends do not know, that the believer is an agnostic too. He is freed from the necessity of having to give an explanation to everything. And more than that, he can stand with the unbeliever in the horror of the uncertainties, unjustness, and meaninglessness of life and can share with him the full lot of being human. If only the Church would meet man where he is in his natural loneliness and despair, and show him that we all stand together and God stands with us, instead of talking of atonement and salvation in language and ideas that are as meaningless as Chinese to a Brazilian peasant! In John Osborne's play, *Look Back in Anger*, the hero, Jimmy Porter, cries out for a cause, but the Church leaves him knee deep in the Sunday papers. Jimmy has 'muscles and guts' for loving, but has to be shown that it matters. But this does not mean that we are to play on men's individual weaknesses and emotions as salvationist preachers like to do. Far from it. We must preach to men in their strength, for both Job and Jimmy Porter have reached positions of strength—Job by his own act, Jimmy Porter by his generation's. Their despair is the frustration of 'man come of age'. For Jimmy Porter, as for Job, 'the systematic answer' has become an evasion and those who offer it irrelevant to his needs. Yet it is always the temptation of the faithful to think that they must know all the answers. Job affirms that knowledge of God and knowledge of all the answers about God are two different things. Man can in fact have only the former—he can only be an agnostic believer.

4

Emmanuel

We have now completed our examination of the Old Testament. First we considered the nature of Israel's pre-exilic law, obedience to which was held to determine her continued election. Here we saw that the law regarded the protection of the person of the individual Israelite as every bit as important as the maintenance of exclusive allegiance to her God. Further, this protection was extended by charitable laws which could never be enforced through the machinery of the courts. This indicated the essentially compassionate nature of the God with whom Israel had to deal. The pre-exilic prophetic protest confirmed our findings, and we particularly noted the prophetic condemnation of entirely appropriate religious practice which was not accompanied by a right attitude to one's neighbour. Faith unaccompanied by works was not only unacceptable, but positively sinful. Then we saw how ancient Israel interpreted the fall of Jerusalem in 586 as God's judgment for her failure to keep the law, and that according to her theologians this should have meant the end of the covenant relationship.

But our examination of the post-exilic material showed how limited was the pre-exilic theology which in effect reduced God's relations with his people to a crude bargain. In fact his nature was such that when it came to the point he could not let Israel go. So by abolishing the concept of communal liability, the post-exilic theologians were able to proclaim a 'new covenant' based solely on the sheer grace of Israel's God. Indeed, in the very act of creation, Israel's election as the chosen people of God had been ensured for all time. Further, it was God's will that all men should enjoy this election by

becoming members of his people through individual acceptance of his law. It was Israel's task as priest-nation to the
world to achieve this. For all men had been made in his
image—that is, for relationship with him.

Finally we investigated the nature of man's relationship
with his God and saw that there must of necessity be an
agnostic element in his belief. Man cannot know all the
answers, though he can know God. This is what ultimately
matters.

Now it is our task to consider in what way Jesus, who
claimed for his Father the God of the Old Testament, confirms our interpretation.

(i)

JESUS AND THE LAW

In his summary of the law, Jesus unequivocally reiterates
the dual concern of Old Testament law:

> 'You shall love the Lord your God with all your heart, and
> with all your soul, and with all your mind. This is the great
> and first commandment. And a second is like it, You shall
> love your neighbour as yourself. On these two command-
> ments depend all the law and the prophets.'
>
> (Matt. 22:37–40)

At no point in his ministry did Jesus seek to set aside the law.
He recognized it as the God-given means whereby order and
harmony were to be maintained within society. No detail was
so unimportant as not to warrant complete obedience:

> 'Think not that I have come to abolish the law and the
> prophets; I have come not to abolish them but to fulfil them.
> For truly, I say to you, till heaven and earth pass away, not
> an iota, not a dot, will pass from the law until all is accom-
> plished.'
>
> (Matt. 5:17–18)

But Jesus recognized the limitations of any legal system. It
could of necessity cover only specific identifiable actions
which could be the subject of legal enforcement through the
courts. But much of the chaos in society results from man's

inner conflicts, his lusts, hates, and jealousies, which lead him to attitudes and actions quite out of sympathy with respect for his neighbour. For Jesus, any thought or action which led to conflict was 'illegal', for it broke the fundamental commandment of love. So in the Sermon on the Mount he reinterprets the ancient laws on murder and adultery (Matt. 5:21–30). To hate a man, to lust after a woman, are equally disorderly. Even to act in self-defence or exercise one's legitimate rights would in itself only further chaos and so is ruled out by Jesus (Matt. 5:38–42). Indeed, under his law his followers have no rights, for they have surrendered, them to the law of love enshrined in the person of Jesus: 'When he was reviled, he did not revile in return; when he suffered, he did not threaten; but he trusted to him who judges justly' (1 Pet. 2:23). So even one's enemies and persecutors are entitled to claim one's love:

> 'You have heard that it was said, "You shall love your neighbour and hate your enemy." But I say to you, Love your enemies and pray for those who persecute you, so that you may be sons of your father who is in heaven; for he makes his sun rise on the evil and on the good, and sends rain on the just and on the unjust. For if you love those who love you, what reward have you? Do not even the tax collectors do the same? And if you salute only your brethren, what more are you doing than others? Do not even the Gentiles do the same? You, therefore, must be perfect, as your heavenly Father is perfect.'
>
> (Matt. 5:43–8)

We have already seen how Old Testament law reflected Israel's understanding of the nature of her God: the same is true of New Testament law. For as Jesus' justification of his law of love indicates, in sustaining men God makes no distinction between good and bad. All have an equal claim on his generosity simply because they are men. It is not God's way to further disorder by disorder. Indeed, he is constantly engaged in the cosmic battle against chaos; though in meeting that chaos head on in the incarnation, death, and resurrection of Jesus, he has shown that ultimately order will prevail.

But nothing brought more disorder to Israelite society than

the love of wealth. Originally conceived as an egalitarian community, by the time of the eighth-century prophets Israel had become the victim of a rapacious class system in which the poor and dependent were ruthlessly exploited. Jesus also recognized that earthly wealth was the greatest single barrier to fulfilling the heavenly law of love:

> 'How hard it is for those who have riches to enter the kingdom of God! For it is easier for a camel to go through the eye of a needle than for a rich man to enter the kingdom of God.' (Luke 18:24–5)

Not that Jesus, any more than ancient Israel, was puritan. But no man could rest content while he knew that others were in want. The rich man at his table had every right to luxuriate in the good things which God had given him: he had no right to do so while Lazarus lay at his gate starving (Luke 16:19–31). How truly Paul wrote when he held that the love of money was the root of all evil. Rather than place his trust in God, man seeks his own security within the created order, and in doing so furthers disorder. But man is not ultimately destined for this world. His enjoyment of possessions here is of necessity transitory. Faced with a choice between the apparent security of his wealth and the equally apparent insecurity of joining the itinerant rabbi from Nazareth, the rich young man imagines that he plays safe (Matt. 19:16–22). But the futility of his action is nicely illustrated by the parable of the farmer who thought he had ensured his future prosperity through a bumper harvest, only to die immediately (Luke 12:16–21). The widow with her mite showed greater perception (Luke 21:1–4). There is in fact nothing more testing of the reality of a man's faith than his attitude towards his property:

> 'Fear not, little flock, for it is your Father's good pleasure to give you the kingdom. Sell your possessions, and give alms; provide yourselves with purses that do not grow old, with a treasure in the heavens that does not fail, where no thief approaches and no moth destroys. For where your treasure is, there will your heart be also.'
>
> (Luke 12:32–4)

The rich young man was clearly a good and attractive person who kept the law and wanted to do the right thing. But this was not so with the religious authorities who, while going through the motions of their faith, yet exploited their fellow men:

> 'Beware of the scribes, who like to go about in long robes, and to have salutations in the market places and the best seats in the synagogues and the places of honour at feasts, who devour widows' houses and for a pretence make long prayers.'
>
> (Mark 12:38–40)

Echoing the eighth-century prophetic protest, Jesus vigorously condemns the scribes and Pharisees for their hypocrisy (Matt. 23:23–39). While they readily fulfil the requirements of the law, they neglect the purpose of law itself, the maintenance of order and harmony within the community. Indeed, just as their fathers rejected the prophets, so they in their turn will do the same, and once again bring catastrophe on Jerusalem (Matt. 24:1–2). Further, the religious authorities are even capable of turning law into anti-law. Thus through spuriously dedicating their property to God, they circumvented the ancient commandment to honour one's parents (Matt. 15:1–9). The frequent conflicts about sabbath observance are similarly to be explained. The sabbath had been given by God as a sign of freedom. Israel was no longer subject to the orders of any political power but only to the divine ordering which God willed for his world. Yet the scribes and Pharisees attempted to use the sabbath rest to perpetuate disorderly situations. In response to their action, Jesus quoted Hosea 6:6: 'I desire mercy, and not sacrifice' (Matt. 12:7). It is not religious practice alone which determines man's acceptance before God, but also his conduct to his fellow men. In fact in their attitude to sabbath observance, the Pharisees showed that they put property before persons, and so rejected the basic principle of the law which they thought they were so scrupulously obeying (Luke 13:10–17).

And Jesus makes it perfectly plain that religion by itself is insufficient:

> 'Not every one who says to me, "Lord, Lord," shall enter the

kingdom of heaven, but he who does the will of my Father
who is in heaven. On that day many will say to me, "Lord,
Lord, did we not prophesy in your name, and cast out
demons in your name, and do many mighty works in your
name?" And then will I declare to them, "I never knew you;
depart from me, you evildoers." '

(Matt. 7:21-3)

No amount of religious activity will make a man acceptable
before God if he fails to fulfil the claims made upon him by
his fellow men. Before he can rightly worship God, such
claims must be met (Matt. 5:23-4). So in the parable of the
sheep and goats, Jesus pictures the last judgment being made
entirely on very ordinary humanitarian grounds—feeding
the hungry, giving drink to the thirsty, clothing the naked,
and visiting the sick and those in prison (Matt. 25:31-46).

And for Jesus there was to be no limit set on those who
could appeal as of right to the exercise of the commandment
to love one's neighbour. For by the parable of the Good
Samaritan, which Luke sets immediately after Jesus' summary
of the law (10:25-37), it is made plain that the 'neighbour'
is no longer to be restricted to one's fellow Israelites, as under
ancient Israel's law, but is to include any human being in
need, simply because he is human.

Jesus thus confirms the attitude of the Old Testament law.
Obedience to God includes love of one's neighbour, now
redefined as man in need. Human welfare is of eternal
significance, whereas personal property is of only transitory
importance. Indeed, it is the mark of the Christian that even
over everyday necessities he should exhibit no anxiety (Matt.
6:25-34).

(ii)

JESUS AND 'THE NEW COVENANT'

Although the post-exilic community of Israel recognized
that God was not bound by a threat theology, that he was
indeed the God of grace, and that that grace was to be

mediated to all men through Israel herself, none the less Israel had no mechanism for dealing with the defaulter, the man who threatened the purity of the community. To protect herself she could only excommunicate him, and so terminate his election as a member of the people of God. But God cannot be so limited: he who has created all, desires all to know his grace, saint and sinner alike. And to make this plain, Jesus broke all customary Jewish practice and deliberately sought the company of those whom Judaism had rejected, the tax-collectors who had thrown in their lot with the occupying Roman authorities, and the sinners whose heinous acts had excluded them from Judaism for all time. Again to justify such action, Matthew makes Jesus quote Hosea 6:6: 'I desire mercy, and not sacrifice' (Matt. 9:13). Orthodox Judaism, instead of fulfilling its mission to the world to bring all men to the knowledge of the one true God, had turned in on itself, concentrating on removing from its ranks all who might contaminate its religious life. But that religious life itself was to be condemned by God as empty for its contemptuous attitude to the spiritual needs of man. Love for the neighbour was to transcend all barriers, for, however sinful, all were made in the image of God and so for relationship with him:

> 'But woe to you, scribes and Pharisees, hypocrites! because you shut the kingdom of heaven against men; for you neither enter yourselves, nor allow those who would enter to go in.'
>
> (Matt. 23:13)

It is not the function of the religious to act as a protection society for God. He is quite capable of looking after himself. Rather it is their function so to eradicate disorder that the kingdom of heaven can come in all its fullness. But the only way that this can be achieved is by love—love which, while still holding fast to the importance of law, yet overrides that law. Such, say both Old and New Testaments, is God's love. We can, then, add a final drawing to our diagram, illustrating the last stage in man's understanding of the nature of the God with whom he has to deal:

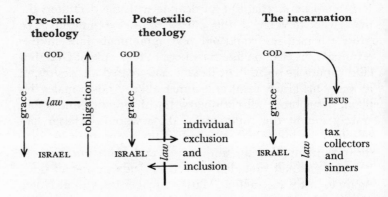

Pre-exilic theology	Post-exilic theology	The incarnation

By his attitude to men like Zacchaeus (Luke 19:1–10) and
the woman who anointed him at Simon's house (Luke
7:36–50), Jesus showed that God's love for man extended far
beyond 'the fence of the law'. There was in fact no point at
which God could let man go, for God is love and can be no
other. Once more Israel's God had been too small.

The particular sin of orthodox Judaism was to forget that
in the end Israel too depended on God's grace. She had not
earned her special position, but received it through God's
election. But because obedience to the law was the sole
criterion for membership of Israel, those who achieved this
tended to think of their position before God as one of right.
They had attained it entirely by their own merit. This
attitude lies behind the parable of the Pharisee and the tax-
collector (Luke 18:9–14). While the Pharisee can stand
unflinchingly before God showing no sense of indebtedness to
him, the tax-collector can only throw himself on God's
mercy. But it is this man who goes home justified for he has
realized that his acceptance by God is entirely due to God's
grace and to no action on his part.

But far from abrogating the law, Jesus, by his reinterpretation of the law in the Sermon on the Mount, showed that in
fact fallen man was incapable of expressing true order and
harmony, which the law was designed to achieve. Being
unable to justify himself before God, he had no alternative

but to fall back on his grace, grace which would not be denied to anyone who asked for it. So in the end both the Pharisee and the tax-collector stood in the same position. They both represented fallen man over against God, and both were dependent on him for their acceptance. But orthodox Judaism, rightly sensing that such revolutionary theology meant the end of its existence, took fright at the full vision of God's love, and crucified it. Yet even this final rebellion of the elect nation could not terminate the covenant of promise. For paradoxically there had been one true Israelite who had fulfilled, as no other man could fulfil, the dual command to love God and his neighbour. It was he who kept the promise of Israel's election alive and who in his person provides the continuity between the Old and New Testaments. So once more God's love triumphs over the dead bones of Israel, and the Israel of 'the new covenant' is born, the Israel of the resurrection body, the Church. Jesus thus fulfils Israel's calling as the suffering servant who makes atonement between God and man (Isa. 53). For through him, our great high priest, all men are seen to be acceptable to God. It is no wonder that the Church took so little time in admitting Gentiles to her ranks. For the barrier of the Jewish law had given way to common dependence on the God of grace.

But it remains religious man's besetting sin to limit God's love. So even today resort is still made to the primitive threat theology of pre-exilic Israel, that refusal to acknowledge God in this life inevitably results in eternal rejection. So God is again made the subject of a crude bargain, men are encouraged to follow him out of fear, not love, and the gospel becomes bad news. But the theology of both Old and New Testaments warns against such specious argument, for both Testaments point to a God who cannot let go, a God who will stop at nothing to bring men into relationship with him. For just when men thought they could draw a line whereby they could limit God's love, they found that God went through and beyond it. So Ezekiel saw God re-create Israel from dry bones; the apostles witnessed the breakdown of the fence of the law. As the hymn puts it:

For the love of God is broader,
   Than the measures of man's mind;
And the heart of the Eternal
   Is most wonderfully kind.

But we make his love too narrow
   By false limits of our own;
And we magnify his strictness
   With a zeal he will not own.[1]

While none of us can know what lies beyond death, it does at least seem reasonable to suppose that God's love remains unlimited and that he will provide himself with the means of continuing to express it to all those who still do not know the fullness of his grace. Indeed, only by doing so can there be that final *shalom*, order and harmony, which is creation's ultimate destiny.

But what are we to do with the threat language—the weeping and gnashing of teeth? It would be a mistake to reject such language out of hand, to say simply that this is part of the Jewish ideas of the time and no longer applicable for 'man come of age'. We must always beware of throwing out the baby with the bath-water. Rather, what we should do is to accept this language as myth in the sense in which biblical scholars use that word—that is, that the language does not refer to something in the future but rather to something in the present, that heaven and hell are not specifically places of the hereafter but can be inhabited in the here and now. In other words, this language describes a present reality, just as that myth of our beginning describes the present reality of our condition—that we are sinners nakedly conscious of our alienation from God. God has, however, shown us that we do not have to remain in this position of alienation: rather, he wishes us to be his sons, and to call him Abba, Father. The Old and New Testaments tell us how he sought to convince man of this fact; but the Old and New Testaments also show that to remain in separation from God can only lead to chaos, to wailing and gnashing of teeth as men exploit men for their own self-gratification. This is the

[1] F. W. Faber, 'There's a wideness in God's mercy,' *English Hymnal* 499.

message of the prophets: it is also the message of Paul. The decision that faces man is, then, vital and immediate: he is called now to turn to the God who wills to embrace him, and so enjoy his love, which is heaven indeed. The alternative is to stay eating the husks thrown to the pigs, which is hell. Recognized as myth, and transferred to the now, the language of heaven and hell has immediate relevance. It is like the rest of the biblical imagery which we associate with becoming a Christian—moving from death to life, from darkness to light. For it is the Christian conviction that only by responding to God's love can man achieve his true potential, his citizenship of heaven, which is his to claim now.

So through the incarnation man discovers the real nature of his relationship to God. In Jesus alone he finds how much he matters to God, that whatever he does the arms of the crucified will not let him go. The picture then of the valley of dry bones is a picture not just for Israel but for each individual, whoever he is, wherever he is, and whatever he has done, into whom the God of grace will yet breathe his re-creating spirit. God is indeed Emmanuel, 'God with us', for in the end he cannot be against us. This is the gospel. It *is* good news.

(iii)

JESUS AND THE NATURE OF MAN'S BELIEF

The author of Job could never have imagined that the test situation which he had envisaged would in fact be lived out. Yet in Jesus this is what happened. So on Golgotha, Jesus, like Job, is placed outside the city, an outcast of that humanity whose true nature he was now to reveal. Of course he has free will, but it is the free will to curse God and die. He doesn't and lives. Jesus' situation is identical to Job's: he is innocent of any fault, yet he is being made to suffer, apparently at the hands of the very God in whom he had trusted and whom he had unflinchingly obeyed. And at the very moment when he is most needed, God remains agonizingly absent. It is in the silence of the absence of God that Jesus is faced with

Job's choice: to deny God or his own integrity. He does neither, but instead affirms both.

But Jesus' affirmation is no simple declaration of faith. He does not resign himself to his fate: instead he argues himself towards his seemingly inevitable death: 'My God, my God, why hast thou forsaken me?' While in Gethsemane he was content to leave it to God, now faced on the one hand with his extinction and on the other with the loss of God's presence, and so of any explanation for what was going on, he, like Job, hurls his hostile 'why?' at the apparently indifferent God. But in that question he neither blasphemes God nor—every bit as important—himself. God is still 'my God'. Yet Jesus makes it unequivocally clear that it is God who is on trial: it is he who has 'forsaken' Jesus. So Jesus continues to express faith, but that faith is phrased as man only can phrase faith: 'In spite of . . . , I believe.' At the point where Jesus exhibits the reality of his humanity, at his death, he also shows what it is to be man—that man cannot of necessity know all the answers, but that he can still believe. He can be an agnostic believer, and this is no contradiction in terms but what it in fact means to be human.

From the earliest days, the Church identified Jesus as the meek suffering servant of Deutero-Isaiah.[1] But we must beware of over-literal identification. While it may be correct to say:

> He was despised and rejected by men;
> a man of sorrows, and acquainted with grief;
> and as one from whom men hide their faces
> he was despised, and we esteemed him not.

(Isa. 53:3)

we cannot continue:

> He was oppressed, and he was afflicted,
> yet he opened not his mouth;
> like a lamb that is led to the slaughter,
> and like a sheep that before its shearers is dumb,
> so he opened not his mouth.

(Isa. 53:7)

[1] M. D. Hooker, *Jesus and the Servant*, London, 1959, raises serious doubts as to whether Jesus himself ever made this identification.

For Jesus' true humanity is not seen in a passionless exhibition of disinterested religion. Jesus is no meek Job of the Prologue content to let events take their course come what may. Rather, like Job of the Dialogue, he wrestles with God and will not let God go until he answers him. But Jesus, unlike Job, has to carry the fight through the jaws of death itself. He has to do that most illogical of all acts, express faith at the point of extinction. So the Light of the World is snuffed out with a question.

But like Job with his self-curse (Job 31), Jesus, by hanging on through death, has forced God's hand. His plea cannot go unanswered: the trial must have a verdict. And this verdict is not that of orthodox Judaism which, acting like Job's three friends, had neglected him as a heretic. It is the verdict of God himself. So God answers from the thunderstorm: the veil of the temple is torn in two. Orthodox Judaism, which had purported to know all the answers, is condemned, and Christ himself vindicated. He rises on the third day. How much of the Evangelists' description of the resurrection events can be accepted literally is a matter of current theological debate. But the reality of the resurrection is there to experience for those who have eyes to see not the empty tomb ('Why do you seek the living among the dead?') but the living Christ ('And he who has seen him, has seen the Father').

It is, then, the cry from the cross that confirms the reality of the incarnation: this was no charade. Jesus does not just go through the motions of what it means to be human, he lives his humanity out in ignorance, futility, and defeat. He shows that under the conditions obtaining in this world, God cannot always get his way. Good men do become the victims of evil. Yet the Church, too embarrassed now to luxuriate in such an earthy feast as Jesus' circumcision, attempts at all levels to mask his manhood, so that paradoxically his divinity can no longer be seen for the tinsel of the Christmas tree. But the meaning of the incarnation is that God knows as man— God takes on the role of Job in the trial (Job 9:32). He becomes the plaintiff who does not, cannot, know all the answers, who must with humanity, questioning humanity, say, 'In spite of . . . , I believe.' But this is not to say that Jesus was mere man—for once one sees the truly human Jesus, one can see God. Jesus raises man to God. So Mary Magdalene encounters a gardener—it is the Lord. The travellers to Emmaus meet a stranger—he is the Lord. The leap of faith still has to be made on the third day, but it must of necessity be made from earth to heaven and not heaven to earth. The author of Ecclesiastes was in the end right:

> Surely there is not a righteous man on earth who does good and never sins.
>
> (7:20)

For when the perfect man appears, he can only be God. But it is as man that Jesus validates his divine nature.

(iv)

'THE GOSPEL' OF THE BIBLE

We have now seen that the New Testament confirms the Old for it reveals the nature of the one unchanging God. His message to us is clear, though its simplicity still surprises us: let God be God, and get on with being man. And increasingly in a world 'come of age' we are able to do this as science exhibits for us the fantasies and facts of human existence. But if we are to enjoy our humanity in all its fullness, we still need to be wise in the Old Testament sense of seeking that order and harmony which God willed for his world at its creation, so that wild and domestic animals can lie down together in peace (*shalom*) and children play in safety by snakes' nests (Isa. 11). Yet we have all eaten of the fruit of the tree of good and evil, and whatever fantasies are exposed and whatever facts are revealed, we are still of necessity faced with making the choice between order and chaos. And it is when we rebel against our human status, when we attempt to establish our own order, when we think we know best (often with the idea of protecting God himself!), that we embrace chaos. The sin of Adam, the sin of the people of Babel with their towers stretching up into heaven, the sin of man through the centuries, believer and atheist alike, is to try and be divine, to be God. And for Christians this refusal

to accept their essential humanity has all too often taken the
peculiarly perverse form of shunning the physical, denying
their flesh and blood. The Marxist jibe that Christians multi-
plied litanies and neglected drains nicely encapsulates this
perversion. But what is the one commandment which Christ
gave us?—to love one another, and nothing is more physical
than love. For to love demands, as any lover knows, our total
involvement in the other—the very guts of our being. Man
indeed can only be man in the full earthiness of his physical
nature. It is this essential earthiness that makes being human
so frightening and from which so many draw back, covering
their fear in pious platitude.

Ibsen's hero, Brand, was a pastor driven by his conscience
to ever-increasing self-denial and sacrifice to the God whom
he sought to serve. Nothing was to stand in the way of his
total commitment. Towards the end of the play,[1] Brand is
asked:

> First, how long shall we have to fight?
> Secondly, how much will it cost us?
> Thirdly, what will be our reward?

Brand's reply is uncompromising:

> How long will you have to fight? Until you die!
> What will it cost? Everything you hold dear.
> Your reward? A new will, cleansed and strong;
> A new faith, integrity of spirit;
> A crown of thorns. That will be your reward.

But Brand had made a terrible mistake. He had forgotten
the nature of the God whom he sought to serve. Terribly he
had denied his own humanity, his own flesh and blood. In
the furtherance of his ministry, he had allowed his son to die,
then his wife—virtually murdered them both—and now as
his own life was about to be engulfed in the falling avalanche
on the mountain he had climbed,[2] he cries in anguish:

> Answer me God, in the moment of death!
> If not by Will, how can man be redeemed?

[1] H. Ibsen, *Brand*, tr. Michael Meyer, New York, 1960, p. 145.
[2] Ibsen, *Brand*, op. cit., p. 157.

The avalanche buries him, filling in the whole valley. A voice cries through the thunder:

He is the God of Love.

As man, we are to be that love—that love in the way in which God is love. And we now know what that is, for God has expressed it through the incarnation, through becoming fully human. Our task then is not to be 'other', more 'beyond', not to go on endlessly up the mountain of denial as Brand did, becoming ever more inaccessible, more alone: no, our task is to stay in the valley down below where there are people, laughter, and sunlight; and sin and suffering too. Our call is to be human, to be man in all his fullness, to sit at table with tarts and crooks and to worry over a widow's poverty. For only by love of life can we affirm life, and only by affirming life shall we be led to ensure that all men have the chance of enjoying that life. We are not summoned to a life of suffering and sacrifice, though this may come our way: rather we are invited to leave the desert with all its deprivations and enter the land of milk and honey, there to feast in plenty. No one loved life more than Jesus. They called him a glutton and a wine-bibber. He enjoyed his Father's creation, luxuriated in it. So are we to luxuriate. For too long Christians have, with Brand, emphasized the safety of denial—but such a theology is as corrupting as the tables of the money-changers. It needs overturning. For what the world is waiting for is a faith which affirms, affirms the goodness of life, affirms love in the very guts of its belly. And it is only as we love life as it should be, that we shall be sufficiently sensitive to appreciate all life's horrors. To affirm life is not to deny the cruelties, injustices, and sheer unfairness of so much that occurs in this world. Rather it is to enter into the cosmic battle to ensure that Christ's kingdom does come, come in all its fullness.

Of course, there will be failure: David must strive in Bathsheba's arms; Peter must deny his Lord; but then they can know the reality of the gracious God who has created them in love, and who in love will not let them go. So they can mirror that same love to others. God does not condemn the man who fails: it is the man who buries his talent for safety who finds himself flung into the dark, the place of wailing and grinding of teeth. For to be human always involves risks, and not all risks come off. Even through no fault of one's own, one can still land on a cross. But in an age seduced into the brothel of success, failure seems as catastrophic as castration. So men play for safety—but no ideal ever had safety for a parent.

And there is no greater ideal than to be human—really human—to expose oneself fully, to love unconditionally. This is no well-intentioned humanism, for it means at the outset recognizing oneself (and all others) as created by God. It can then only be achieved, as Jesus—the one perfect man—showed, by total fellowship with God, in utter dependence upon him. In this life we know that sin prevents our fully realizing our perfection—yet the command remains: You shall be holy; for I the Lord your God am holy (Lev. 19:2). You shall be those who bring wholeness, harmony, and order in all you do and say and think. For the land of milk and honey can only be entered if man co-operates with the God who wills his entry. The Christian is not called to make a choice between God and the world. Rather he is to affirm both, and in fellowship with his Creator enjoy his creation, whose true order is his to discover and proclaim. So let God be God, and get on with being man.

The Decalogue

The Decalogue as set out in Exod. 20:1–17 reads:
  And God spoke all these words, saying,
  'I am the Lord your God, who brought you out of the land of Egypt, out of the house of bondage.
 1. You shall have no other gods before me.
 2. You shall not make for yourself a graven image, or any likeness of anything that is in heaven above, or that is in the earth beneath, or that is in the water under the earth; you shall not bow down to them or serve them; for I the Lord your God am a jealous God, visiting the iniquity of the fathers upon the children to the third and the fourth generation of those who hate me, but showing steadfast love to thousands of those who love me and keep my commandments.
 3. You shall not take the name of the Lord your God in vain; for the Lord will not hold him guiltless who takes his name in vain.
 4. Remember the sabbath day, to keep it holy. Six days you shall labour, and do all your work; but the seventh day is a sabbath to the Lord your God; in it you shall not do any work, you, or your son, or your daughter, your manservant, or your maidservant, or your cattle, or the sojourner who is within your gates; for in six days the Lord made heaven and earth, the sea, and all that is in them, and rested the seventh day; therefore the Lord blessed the sabbath day and hallowed it.
 5. Honour your father and your mother, that your days may be long in the land which the Lord your God gives you.
 6. You shall not kill.
 7. You shall not commit adultery.
 8. You shall not steal.
 9. You shall not bear false witness against your neighbour.

10. You shall not covet your neighbour's house; you shall not covet your neighbour's wife, or his manservant, or his maidservant, or his ox, or his ass, or anything that is your neighbour's.'

The Decalogue is also set out at Deut. 5:6–21. The two major variations occur in the fourth and tenth commandments:

4. Observe the sabbath day, to keep it holy, as the Lord your God commanded you. Six days you shall labour, and do all your work; but the seventh day is a sabbath to the Lord your God; in it you shall not do any work, you, or your son, or your daughter, or your manservant, or your maidservant, or your ox, or your ass, or any of your cattle, or the sojourner who is within your gates, that your manservant, and your maidservant may rest as well as you. You shall remember that you were a servant in the land of Egypt, and the Lord your God brought you out thence with a mighty hand and an outstretched arm; therefore the Lord your God commanded you to keep the sabbath day.

10. Neither shall you covet your neighbour's wife; and you shall not desire your neighbour's house, his field, or his manservant, or his maidservant, his ox, or his ass, or anything that is your neighbour's.

Chronological Table

Date	Event	Kings	Prophets
1000		David (1000–961)	Nathan
	On Solomon's death separate kingdoms of Israel in the north (capital Samaria) and Judah in the south (capital Jerusalem) formed	Solomon (c. 961–922)	

*　*　*　*　*

Date	Event	Kings	Prophets
750			Amos Hosea
721	Fall of Samaria to Assyrians and end of the northern kingdom of Israel	Hezekiah (715–687)	Isaiah Micah
		Josiah (640–609)	
621	Discovery of law book in the temple led to the Deuteronomic reform		Jeremiah

Date	Event	Kings	Prophets
586	Fall of Jerusalem, destruction of the temple, and exile in Babylon of king and leading citizens		Ezekiel
561	Release of Jehoiachin from prison		
538	Edict of Persian king, Cyrus, allowing Jews to return from exile		Deutero-Isaiah

Index of Biblical References